STRATEGIC INDICATORS FOR

FOR

HIGHER EDUCATION

EDUCATION

Improving
Performance

STRATEGIC INDICATORS FOR HIGHER EDUCATION

FOR

HIGHER EDUCATION

Improving
Performance

Barbara E. Taylor
Joel W. Meyerson and
William F. Massy

Peterson's Guides
Princeton, New Jersey

Library of Congress Cataloging-in-Publication Data

Taylor, Barbara E.
    Strategic indicators in higher education : improving performance / Barbara E. Taylor, Joel W. Meyerson, William F. Massy.
        p.   cm.
    ISBN 1-56079-179-9 : $49.95
    1. Universities and colleges—United States—Evaluation Statistics. 2. Universities and colleges—United States Finance—Statistics. 3. Educational indicators—United States. I. Meyerson, Joel W., 1951–   . II. Massy, William F. III. Title.
LB2331.62.T39   1993
378.73'021—dc20   93-15727
                                                                   CIP

Composition and design by Peterson's Guides

Printed in the United States of America

10 9 8 7 6 5 4 3 2 1

Table of Contents

Preface

There is a real and deepening crisis in American higher education that threatens the quality and diversity of the system. Ultimately, the quality of education available for our students—and necessary to support our national economy and social system—may be at risk. The need for more effective leadership has been apparent for the past three decades as higher education has experienced rapid growth and then serious financial setbacks. Colleges and universities have become incredibly complex organizations, and, as a result, many boards and administrators oversee institutions that have become billion-dollar businesses with thousands of employees, huge physical plants, and increasingly diverse missions. Even a small college can be as complex as the average private corporation.

Without dramatic improvements in the way governing boards and college and university management interact as well as tend to their own responsibilities, our schools will falter in greater numbers than ever before. Boards and administrators must proactively provide the leadership and guidance that the times demand, and this requires better, more meaningful information. Governance is decision-making, and decisions can be no better than the quality of information available to inform them. What is missing for most boards and administrators is reliable, strategic, comparative information that can help them understand the condition of their institution relative to peers and enable them to formulate improved policies and strategies. *Strategic Indicators* is the most comprehensive source of comparative information available. It will illuminate institutional condition in four key resource areas: financial, intellectual, physical, and information. Using this volume, boards and administrators, working together, can understand more fully how their institution is performing relative to peers and how leadership can respond more effectively.

The guidance *Strategic Indicators* provides will enable trustees and administrators to be more effective and informed institutional leaders and will allow administrators to work more productively with their boards in their shared effort to ensure long-term institutional effectiveness and vitality. No task facing higher education's leadership can be more important.

Robert Conway
Trustee
University of Notre Dame

Introduction

The role of governing boards and the expectations boards and managers have of one another are changing. These changes, conceived in corporate boardrooms, are sweeping higher education as well.

One need only witness the corporate upheavals of the early 1990s to understand that a fundamental restructuring of the relationship between management and boards is in process. At major firms like IBM, General Motors, American Express, and Westinghouse, boards under fire from institutional shareholders unhappy with lagging corporate performance have ousted their chief executives. Boards themselves have been criticized for being too complacent for too long, concerned more about their own comfort and perquisites than the condition of the companies they govern.

In higher education pressure to restructure and reform is being applied not by stockholders but by public opinion and a climate of economic uncertainty and decline that is unlikely to moderate very much in the foreseeable future. Many institutions, including even the best managed and most well-heeled, are experiencing unprecedented levels of financial distress. Some are planning for multiple-year deficits for the first time. Many are being forced to scale back programs and personnel.

Why is this happening? The economy is fluctuating under pressure from a rising national debt, an unfavorable balance of trade, unemployment and lagging wages, and demands for public spending in areas such as law enforcement, public services, and health care. Higher education has more competition for scarce resources and in most states is losing to other priorities. Along with public institutions, private higher education is feeling the pinch as financial aid programs and other forms of public revenue erode.

At the same time, costs continue to rise. Some colleges and universities have struggled to increase productivity through technology or by downsizing their programs and services. Students and families are finding it increasingly difficult to afford rising college costs.

The nation's demographic profile is also changing dramatically. Each year increasing numbers of traditional college-age students will be found among minority, immigrant, and disadvantaged groups that most colleges and universities have little history of serving effectively.

Public expectations of higher education are increasing as institutions are seen as engines for economic development and social reform. But at the same time, higher education's well-publicized academic and leadership shortcomings have left many citizens and policymakers skeptical about the ability of the enterprise to rise to the challenges society faces.

Some of these factors are beyond any institution's control; others can be influenced. Together they are creating one of the most challenging environments American higher education has ever faced.

In response to these challenges, increasing numbers of boards are playing a more active role in guiding their institutions. Through their interactions with management, they are helping colleges and universities curb random growth, rein in spiraling costs, and stem institutional drift. Indeed, they are helping to create *strategically focused* institutions committed to achieving distinctive competence in core programs today and to attaining essential institutional goals in the future. To accomplish this, boards and managers are *thinking strategically*—defining a vision, setting institutional priorities, balancing current and future needs, and monitoring institutional performance.

Strategic thinking requires objectivity, an honest assessment of how an institution is doing and where it is heading—that is, its strategic position. This is where *Strategic Indicators for Higher Education* comes in. *Strategic Indicators* is the successor to two pioneering studies published by the Association of Governing Boards of Universities and Colleges—*Strategic Analysis: Using Comparative Data to Understand Your Institution* and *Strategic Decision Making: Key Questions and Indicators for Trustees*. All three books are based on the use of **indicators**, which are ratios, percentages, or other quantitative values that allow an institution to compare its position in key strategic areas to peers, to past performance, or to previously set goals.

In commerce and economics, common indicators include earnings per share, return on investment, and market share. In higher education one is apt to hear about indicators such as student-faculty ratio, yield on endowment, and percentage of applicants accepted for admission. In either case the use is the same. Indicators enable decision-makers to assess an institution's strategic position through comparative analysis.

Many institutions find it extremely difficult to conduct this kind of analysis because they lack timely, reliable information on key strategic values from comparable institutions. *Strategic Indicators* responds to this need by analyzing over 90 key indicators based on data collected from more than 700 institutions. It provides detailed descriptions of more than 70 indicators as well as comparative data on nearly 20 more.

In selecting indicators, we were governed by the following tenet: Since trustees and other institutional leaders do not have the time to analyze all (or even most) available information, they must focus on areas most likely to affect the success of their institution—that is, those that will influence its performance and strategic position over the long term. These *critical success factors* will not be the same for all institutions but will vary depending on size, control, location, history, mission, goals, and other factors. For example, a nonselective, tuition-dependent private college will avidly monitor applications, acceptances, and "yield" (the percentage of accepted applicants who matriculate). A research university will watch trends and composition of sponsored research dollars. A public community college that wants to increase the proportion of graduates who transfer to four-year institutions will monitor that indicator.

Included among the indicators in this book are many of the measures institutions will want to monitor, but this is not an exhaustive list. The diversity of the higher education enterprise is such that no single listing of indicators could reflect comprehensively the condition of all institutions with their varying circumstances, missions, and strategies. For example, a church-related college may wish to watch the percentage of total revenues provided by the sponsoring denomination, an indicator not provided in this book. Readers should begin with the indicators provided here and then ask themselves, "What else do we need to know in order to understand the condition of our institution?"

How to Use Strategic Indicators

Strategic Assets. A powerful method of analyzing strategic performance is to perceive an institution as comprising four fundamental *strategic assets*. These are:

- Financial capital
- Physical capital
- Information capital
- Human capital

Financial capital is an institution's economic resources—its revenue and reserves, investments, and endowment. **Physical capital** consists of buildings, land, and equipment. **Information capital** is library and computer resources. And **human capital** is an institution's intellectual wealth—its students, faculty, and staff. The size and quality of these assets—and the *relationships* among them—drive an institution's strategic condition.

Strategic Indicators. For each type of strategic asset, we have selected a number of key *strategic indicators* that capture the meaning and value of that area. Some indicators are more accurate measures than others. For instance, financial indicators such as endowment yield and tuition and fee income per student are precise and reliable. Others are less so but serve as acceptable proxies for the desired information. For example, we have used as an indicator of deferred maintenance the ratio of the estimated maintenance backlog to the total replacement value of plant. Both the maintenance backlog and the replacement value of plant are inexact measures, but we believe the ratio is a useful and easily calculated indicator of the condition of physical-plant condition. Generally, we chose indicators that are well understood, widely accepted, and easy to compute using data readily available to most institutions.

Included in *Strategic Indicators* are key indicators in the following areas:

- **Financial capital**
  Revenue structure
  Expenditure structure
  Resources and reserves
  Endowment and investments
  Development
- **Physical capital**
  Plant and equipment
- **Information capital**
  Library
  Computing
- **Human capital**
  Students
  Enrollment
  Tuition and financial aid
  Faculty and staff
  Research

Comparisons. To assess strategic performance and position, it is often helpful to compare a college or university with similar institutions. We collected and analyzed data for six separate "peer" groups—three each for public and private institutions.

- Public
    Two-year colleges
    Regional colleges and universities
    Research and Land-Grant universities

- Private
    Tuition and fees less than $7,500
    Tuition and fees between $7,500 and $10,000
    Tuition and fees more than $10,000

These groupings have allowed apt comparisons in recent studies, and most are self-explanatory. However, two require clarification. Public *regional colleges and universities* include institutions eligible for membership in the American Association of State Colleges and Universities (AASCU). Public *research and Land-Grant universities* include institutions eligible for membership in the National Association of State Universities and Land-Grant Colleges (NASULGC) or the Association of American Universities (AAU).

Analysis. Each strategic indicator in the main part of the book is accompanied by a *narrative* and a *visual* analysis. The narrative analysis (1) details the significance of each indicator, (2) interprets the findings for each peer group, and (3) poses questions trustees and other decision-makers might ask about that area. The visual analysis arrays for each peer group the median indicator value along with percentile distributions. Where it is more appropriate or useful to display the indicator through a pie chart, table, or other device, we do so.

The median represents the midpoint value in a distribution, with an equal number of values above and below it. The median often is a more useful measure of central tendency than the mean, which can be misleading if a distribution contains a few very low or very high values. We show in the graphs the fifth, fiftieth, and ninety-fifth percentiles. The fiftieth is the median, and the other percentiles reflect the range of values absent any outliers. In pie charts and tables, other values are displayed as warranted.

Before beginning...some advice and caveats are in order.

In starting out, a board and administration may want to analyze as many applicable indicators as possible in order to identify current or potential problem areas for the institution. Subsequently, institutional leaders can develop a shorter list of measures that must be monitored continuously or periodically, either because they suggest the institution is at risk in some way or because they are deemed essential to the achievement of the institution's strategy.

It is important to note that there is no "right" or "wrong" value for any indicator. What is essential is to know an institution's position relative to peers, to past performance, or to goals, and then to understand the reasons for any disparities noted.

The data presented here are national norms for broadly defined peer groups. An institution may want to collect and analyze comparative data for other kinds of peer groups, such as the institutions with which it competes for students, fellow colleges and universities in a state system, or institutions that are affiliated with a common religious denomination.

In addition to analyzing comparative institutional data, it is important to bear in mind the external trends and influences not directly reflected in the indicators presented here. For example, public universities must monitor political and economic trends in the state that will affect appropriations. Community colleges must monitor local business trends for clues about needed new programs. Religiously affiliated colleges must study trends in church membership and denominational support for higher education.

Caveats notwithstanding, *Strategic Indicators* provides a framework for understanding institutional condition and taking steps to improve competitive position.

- We begin by describing the ten most critical indicators, those that the majority of institutions will want to assess first and monitor regularly.
- The body of the book presents all the major indicators (including full discussions of the top ten indicators). You will find in these pages a description of each indicator, an analysis of the peer group data, a short list of questions trustees and top administrators might ask to understand their institution's condition with respect to that indicator, and a graphic display of the data.
- The section called Additional Indicators (pages 135-158) presents 23 additional indicators in graphic form only.
- The chapter "Notes on the Survey" describes the methodology of the study used to collect the data.

The Top Ten Indicators

Some indicators may be more revealing than others for a particular institution. For example, a research university will want to monitor trends in research funding, while a liberal arts college desiring to increase the diversity of its student body will wish to track enrollments by race and ethnicity. Still, for most institutions a handful of indicators will be especially revealing and hence especially important to monitor. Despite vast differences among institutions, the indicators that follow may form the core of many institutions' "to watch" list.

1. **Overall Revenue Structure**. All institutions need to understand where their revenues come from, note how stable and reliable those sources have been over time, and estimate future trends. See page 2.

2. **Overall Expenditure Structure**. Institutions must know where they are spending their resources, what their expenditure trends are, and what these trends suggest about future financial stability. See page 16.

3. **Excess (Deficit) of Current Fund Revenues Over Current Fund Expenditures.** This indicator reflects the degree to which an institution is living within its means. Current funds are those available to meet operating needs in a given year. When revenues exceed expenditures, an institution has resources that can be added to reserves or used for other purposes, such as capital investment. However, when expenditures exceed revenues, the shortfall must be covered by borrowing or drawing from reserves. Continuing shortfalls can lead to the financial failure of the institution. See page 24.

4. **Percent of Freshman Applicants Accepted and Percent of Accepted Freshmen Who Matriculate**. While treated as two separate measures in this book, these indicators are highly interrelated. The first is a measure of institutional selectivity that is crucial for all but open admissions colleges. An institution that accepts a large or growing proportion of applicants may have less control over student quality and, eventually, the overall size of the student body. The second indicator, a measure of admissions "yield," is an important indicator of an institution's attractiveness, which, with selectivity, suggests how much flexibility it has to control the quality and composition of its own student body. See pages 82 and 84.

5. **Ratio of Full-Time Equivalent Students to Full-Time Equivalent Faculty**. While an institution's overall ratio of students to faculty may mask significant variability among programs and departments, this measure is the starting point for assessing faculty workload and productivity. See page 106.

6. **Institutional Grant Aid as a Percent of Tuition and Fee Income**. This measure of net tuition income reflects the extent to which the institution in effect returns a percentage of tuition income in the form of grant aid. The measure is especially important for the private sector but is becoming increasingly significant for public institutions as their tuitions rise. See page 88.

7. **Tenure Status of Full-Time Equivalent Faculty**. This measure suggests how much flexibility the institution has to add faculty in areas of growing student demand or to decrease the size of the faculty if enrollments or revenues decline. See page 102.

8. **Percent of Total Full-Time Equivalent Employees Who Are Faculty**. This indicator reflects an institution's mission and program mix as well as its choices about the division of labor between faculty and staff. A large or growing proportion

of faculty may indicate an appropriate emphasis on the academic mission, or it might suggest that the institution is giving insufficient attention to administrative and support functions. See page 116.

9. **Maintenance Backlog as a Percent of Total Replacement Value of Plant**. Deferred maintenance is a growing concern for most institutions, whose capital assets are deteriorating as scarce funds are diverted to academic and other priorities that may seem more pressing. See page 64.

10. **Percent of Living Alumni Who Have Given at Any Time During the Past Five Years**. Alumni giving is a significant source of institutional support and an important proxy for constituent opinion about institutional performance. The measure has always been significant for private colleges and universities; and as public institutions become more dependent on private giving, it is becoming increasingly significant for them as well. See page 56.

Financial Capital

Financial capital is a crucial indication of an institution's overall health; academic excellence cannot be achieved without strong financial resources. Major financial indicators include overall revenue structure, overall expenditure structure, endowments and investments, resources and reserves, and development. Institutions can monitor such indicators with a goal of attaining long-range financial equilibrium, in which the rate of revenue growth equals or exceeds expenditure growth. These indicators are also useful for monitoring various sources and types of revenue, with the goal of achieving a diversified revenue structure based on independent fund sources.

Overall Revenue Structure

SIGNIFICANCE

Revenue structure measures the diversity of funding sources and the volatility of income streams. Generally, an institution that derives its revenue from several independent sources enjoys greater flexibility and stability. By contrast, dependence on one or a very few sources—such as tuition—may result in greater financial volatility and unpredictability. Institutions that primarily derive their revenue from only a few sources may have the opportunity to increase income and stability by developing new revenue sources.

INTERPRETATION

Public institutions, in many respects, have more diversified revenue structures than private institutions. In addition to state appropriations, many public institutions receive significant funding from federal and local governments. Public funding, however, can be very volatile, particularly during times of economic duress and regional recessions. Significantly, tuition and fees constitute an increasing source of revenue for public institutions, exceeding 20 percent of the total revenue structure at many institutions. For private institutions, tuition and fees are the most prominent revenue sources, representing more than half the total revenue for most institutions. Private giving and endowment income also constitute an important revenue stream, accounting for 5 to 15 percent of revenue at most private institutions. Federal grants and contracts tend to represent a larger share of the revenue structure for public institutions than for private institutions.

Revenue Structure

Source	Public Two-year	Public Regional Colleges and Universities AASCU	Public Research and Land-Grant Universities NASULGC	Private Tuition under $7,500	Private Tuition $7,500-$10,000	Private Tuition over $10,000
Tuition and fees	21%	22%	17%	51%	59%	59%
Federal appropriations	--	--	2	2	--	--
State appropriations	38	46	38	--	--	--
Local appropriations	14	--	1	--	--	--
Federal grants and contracts	9	8	13	8	4	4
State grants and contracts	4	2	2	2	3	2
Local grants and contracts	1	--	--	--	--	--
Private gifts, grants, and contracts	1	2	4	14	8	7
Endowment support	--	--	--	6	3	5
Sales and services of educational activities	--	1	3	--	1	1
Sales and services of auxiliary	7	15	11	13	15	16
Other services*	4	3	9	4	6	6

*Other includes revenue from hospitals, independent operations, other sources, etc.

A note about this table. Numbers in this table are numerical averages, or means, in contrast to medians, which are used elsewhere in the book. In a perfectly normal distribution, the median and mean are the same. Where a distribution is highly skewed, the two values may be very different. Hence, the reader will note differences, occasionally extreme, between the values in this table and those found on succeeding pages, where medians of some of the variables that comprise this table are displayed.

QUESTIONS

1. What are our most significant sources of revenue, and how do they compare to our peer institutions?
2. For private institutions, how dependent are we on tuition; for public institutions, how dependent are we on state appropriations? Is this dependence increasing or decreasing over time?
3. What will our revenue structure likely be in five years? What sources are likely to increase; what sources are likely to decrease? How are we preparing for this change?
4. What new revenue sources have we identified? What are our plans for developing these sources?

Tuition and Fees as a Percent of Total Revenue

PUBLIC

SIGNIFICANCE

Tuition and fees are the primary source of revenue for private institutions. Increasingly, they are a significant source of revenue for public institutions, which are instituting or increasing charges. Excessive tuition dependence increases volatility, particularly during economic recession and times of demographic change and uncertainty.

INTERPRETATION

Virtually all private institutions are tuition driven. Tuition and fees represent, on average, about 60 percent of total revenue for mid- and higher-priced private institutions and about one half of total revenue for lower-priced private institutions. For public institutions, tuition and fees are also significant—they constitute about one fifth of revenue for two-year and public regional colleges and universities and about 15 percent for research and Land-Grant universities.

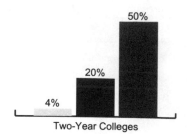

Two-Year Colleges

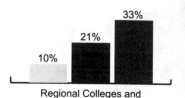

Regional Colleges and Universities

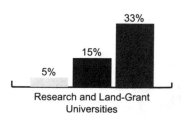

Research and Land-Grant Universities

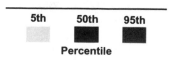

5th 50th 95th

Percentile

PRIVATE

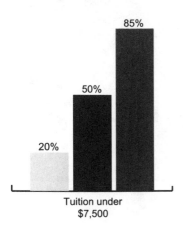

Tuition under
$7,500

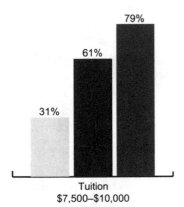

Tuition
$7,500–$10,000

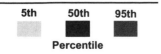

Tuition over
$10,000

5th   50th   95th
Percentile

QUESTIONS

1. What percent of our total revenue is attributable to tuition and fees, and how does this compare to our peer institutions? How "deep" are these revenue sources?
2. Is our dependence on tuition and fees increasing or decreasing over time?
3. Is our enrollment stable? Are changes in enrollment creating volatility in tuition and fees revenue?
4. By what amount have we increased tuition and fees in recent years? Can we expect to increase tuition and fees in the future?
5. What percent of our total revenue is tuition and fees likely to represent during the next five years?

State Appropriations as a Percent of Total Revenue (Public Institutions Only)

SIGNIFICANCE

State appropriations are the primary source of funding for public institutions. (States appropriate virtually no resources for direct use of private institutions.) State appropriations to public institutions have been declining or growing at a slower rate than in prior years, even as enrollment has swelled. This is due to the impact of the recession on state revenues, the transfer of many formerly federal obligations to the states, and competition for state funds. Public institutions are compensating for this shortfall through strategies such as raising tuition and fees, reducing programs, and cutting personnel.

INTERPRETATION

State appropriations to public institutions range, on average, from about 37 percent of total revenue for two-year colleges, to nearly 40 percent for research and Land-Grant universities, to over 45 percent for public regional colleges and universities. Two-year institutions fund many of their activities through user fees and other charges, and research and Land-Grant universities receive significant support for research and related activities.

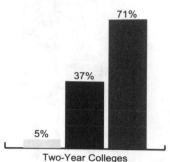

Two-Year Colleges

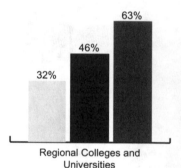

Regional Colleges and Universities

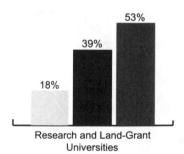

Research and Land-Grant Universities

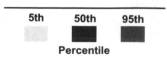

Percentile

QUESTIONS

1. What percent do state appropriations represent of total revenue, and how does this compare to our peer institutions?
2. Are state appropriations increasing or decreasing over time? What are the prospects for the future?
3. What is the nature of our relationship with the state? Are we actively working to enhance this relationship and future funding?
4. What are our plans for dealing with declining or inadequate state appropriations? What other revenue sources are we developing?

Federal Grants and Contracts as a Percent of Total Revenue

PUBLIC

SIGNIFICANCE

Most basic research in the United States is conducted by colleges and universities, and most of this research is funded by federal grants and contracts. Although federal funding for research has been growing at a slower rate recently, it still comprises a significant part of the revenue structure for many institutions. Institutions are compensating for shortfalls in federal research funding with grants and contracts from corporations and by supporting research with institutional funds.

INTERPRETATION

Federal grants and contracts are a factor for all types of institutions and account, on average, for about 5 percent of total revenue. This level is significantly higher at public institutions, exceeding 10 percent for the average research and Land-Grant university. Percentages are lower for private institutions, although they exceed 6 percent for lower-priced institutions.

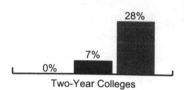

Two-Year Colleges

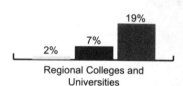

Regional Colleges and Universities

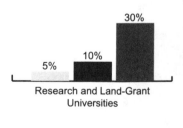

Research and Land-Grant Universities

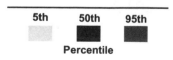

| 5th | 50th | 95th |

Percentile

PRIVATE

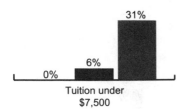

31%

6%

0%

Tuition under
$7,500

QUESTIONS

1. What percent of total revenue is attributable to federal grants and contracts, and how does this compare to our peer institutions?
2. Have federal grants and contracts increased or decreased over the years?
3. How much of federal grant and contract revenue represents indirect cost recovery? Do these collections approximate our full average costs? Do they exceed our estimated incremental indirect costs (that is, the cost of supplying the extra facilities and services needed to support the federal research program)?
4. What other sources are available to fund research? Are corporations sponsoring more research? Are we internally funding more research than previously?
5. What are our plans to fund research in the future if federal grants and contracts do not increase or decline?

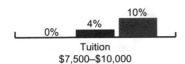

10%

4%

0%

Tuition
$7,500–$10,000

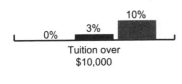

10%

3%

0%

Tuition over
$10,000

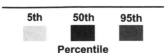

| 5th | 50th | 95th |

Percentile

Private Gifts, Grants, and Contracts as a Percent of Total Revenue

SIGNIFICANCE

Private gifts, grants, and contracts represent all revenue from private sources—individuals, foundations, corporations—expended on operations. This revenue is an important source of diversity and stability in the revenue structure of many institutions.

INTERPRETATION

Private gifts, grants, and contracts represent, on average, over 4 percent of total revenue. The level of private revenue is substantially greater for private institutions than public institutions. For example, private revenue accounts for over 12 percent of total revenue for the average lower-priced private institution. This is likely attributable to the historical need of private institutions to identify and develop diverse sources of revenue.

Two-Year Colleges

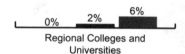

Regional Colleges and Universities

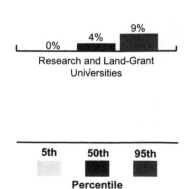

Research and Land-Grant Universities

5th	50th	95th

Percentile

PRIVATE

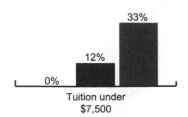

Tuition under
$7,500

QUESTIONS

1. What percent of our total revenue is from private gifts, grants, and contracts, and how does this compare with our peer institutions?
2. What are our sources of private revenue? Are private gifts, grants, and contracts increasing or decreasing over time?
3. How much private revenue do we expect to receive five years from now? What are our plans for increasing private revenue in the future?

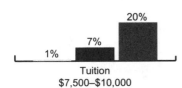

Tuition
$7,500–$10,000

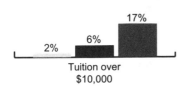

Tuition over
$10,000

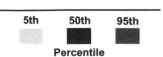

Percentile

Endowment Support for Operations as a Percent of Total Revenue

PUBLIC

SIGNIFICANCE

Institutions usually expend a substantial portion of endowment return on current operations. Endowment support is generally unrestricted and is used to enhance academic programs and activities. The amount expended is determined by the "spending policy" set by the governing board. Spending policy should balance the current and future economic needs of the institution.

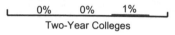

Two-Year Colleges

INTERPRETATION

Endowment provides relatively little support for operations, especially in public institutions. For private institutions, on average, endowment support represents between 2 and 3 percent of total revenue. Even at the better-endowed private institutions, endowment rarely contributes more than 10 percent to operations. For the limited number of institutions with large endowments, endowments are more likely to be a bulwark against future difficulty than a major contributor to operating revenue.

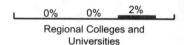

Regional Colleges and Universities

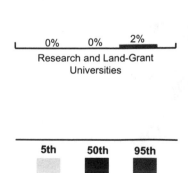

Research and Land-Grant Universities

PRIVATE

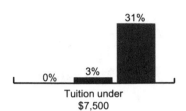

**Tuition under
$7,500**

QUESTIONS
1. What percent of our total revenue is attributable to endowment support, and how does this compare to our peer institutions?
2. Is the level of endowment support for operations adequate?
3. What is our "spending policy"? How has it changed over time? How do we determine what portion of endowment return will be expended on current operations?

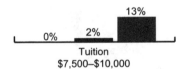

**Tuition
$7,500–$10,000**

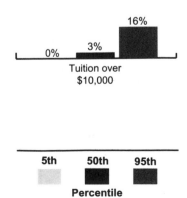

**Tuition over
$10,000**

Sales and Services of Auxiliaries as a Percent of Total Revenue

PUBLIC

SIGNIFICANCE

Auxiliary services provide an increasingly important source of revenue for many institutions. As a general rule, institutions should assure that auxiliaries are not losing money; more frequently, however, auxiliary services generate net revenue for an institution. Institutions have learned how to profitably manage—or outsource—a wide variety of operations, including dining services, print shops, and bookstores.

INTERPRETATION

Auxiliary services, on average, provide about 10 percent of total revenue in public institutions. The percentages are somewhat higher for private institutions, with auxiliaries contributing about 15 percent to revenue.

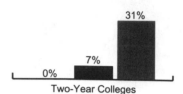

Two-Year Colleges

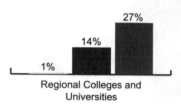

Regional Colleges and Universities

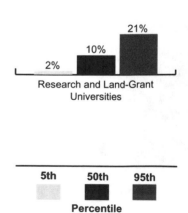

Research and Land-Grant Universities

5th 50th 95th
Percentile

PRIVATE

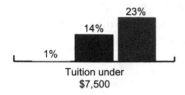

23%

14%

1%

Tuition under
$7,500

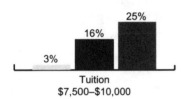

25%

16%

3%

Tuition
$7,500–$10,000

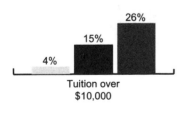

26%

15%

4%

Tuition over
$10,000

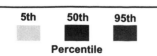

5th   50th   95th

Percentile

Overall Expenditure Structure

SIGNIFICANCE

Expenditure structure shows how an institution disperses its funds to purchase goods and services to support current operations. While the same expenditure categories are used by virtually all institutions, patterns of expenditure vary somewhat from one kind of institution to another, based largely on institutional mission, wealth, and control (public versus private). For a given instittuion, changes in expenditure structure over time can provide evidence of financial strength or vulnerability. For example, growing expenditures for financial aid may signal dificulty in attracting sufficient numbers of full-pay students, while declines in plant operation and maintenance expenditures may suggest that deferred maintenance is rising.

INTERPRETATION

The most sizable expenditure for all institutional categories is instruction, which accounts for approximately 30 percent of expenses overall and more than 40 percent in public two-year colleges. Among other significant expenditure areas are institutionally funded scholarships, especially in the private sector, where they account for between 15 and 18 percent of expenditures, and among public two-year colleges, which serve many low income students. Institutional support, which includes most administrative expenses (except academic administration), and auxiliary enterprises are also major expenditures for most institutions. An exception to the last of these items is two-year public colleges, where dormitories and similar auxiliary functions associated with residential institutions are less common. Student services, academic support, and plant expenses also consume sizable resources at most institutions. Only at public research and Land-Grant universities do expenditures for sponsored research exceed 1 or 2 percent.

Expenditure Structure

Source	Public Two-year	Public Regional Colleges and Universities AASCU	Public Research and Land-Grant Universities NASULGC	Private Tuition under $7,500	Private Tuition $7,500-$10,000	Private Tuition over $10,000
Instruction	43%	36%	33%	27%	28%	30%
Sponsored research	0	3	13	0	1	1
Public service	8	4	7	1	1	1
Academic support	5	8	8	5	6	6
Libraries[1]	2	3	3	3	3	3
Computing[1]	1	1	1	1	1	1
Student services	10	7	5	9	9	8
Institutional support	12	11	8	18	13	14
Plant operations and maintenance	10	8	7	10	8	8
Scholarships & fellowships	11	6	9	15	18	18
Auxiliary services	2	14	10	10	13	13
Faculty medical practice[2]	0	0	1	0	0	0
Hospitals	0	0	1	0	0	2
Independent Operations	0	2	0	4	4	1

[1]Included in Academic Support
[2]Included in Auxiliary Services

A note about this table. Numbers in this table are numerical averages, or means, in contrast to medians, which are used elsewhere in the book. In a perfectly normal distribution, the median and mean are the same. Where a distribution is highly skewed, the two values may be very different. Hence, the reader will note differences, sometimes extreme, between the values in this table and those found on succeeding pages, where medians of some of the variables that comprise this table are displayed.

Instructional Expenditures as a Percent of Total Current Fund Expenditures

SIGNIFICANCE

The proportion of total expenditures devoted to instruction may reflect an institution's commitment to academic quality. Institutions are becoming more complex, and there are myriad demands on resources. Generally, institutions that preserve a significant portion of their budgets for instruction are investing in academic excellence today and for the future.

INTERPRETATION

On average, private institutions spend just under one third of total current expenditures for instruction. This amount is relatively constant for all types of private institutions, though it is greatest in high-tuition schools. Public institutions generally spend between 30 percent and 40 percent on instruction. For both public and private institutions, the gap between schools that spend more and those that spend less on instruction is relatively narrow.

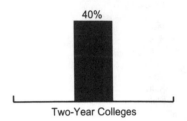

Two-Year Colleges

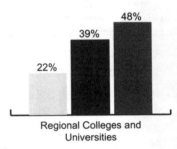

Regional Colleges and Universities

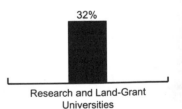

Research and Land-Grant Universities

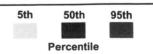

5th	50th	95th

Percentile

PRIVATE

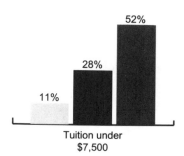

11% 28% 52%

Tuition under $7,500

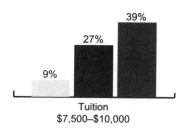

9% 27% 39%

Tuition $7,500–$10,000

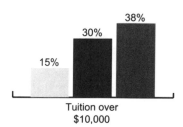

15% 30% 38%

Tuition over $10,000

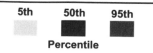

| 5th | 50th | 95th |

Percentile

Instructional Expenditures per FTE Student

SIGNIFICANCE

The amount of dollars actually expended on instruction often correlates with an institution's academic quality. Instructional expenditures per student measures the amount of resources devoted to the core mission of an institution—teaching and related activities. Although per-student instructional expenditures are a measure of quality, institutions must use instructional resources effectively and efficiently.

INTERPRETATION

Public research and Land-Grant universities and higher-priced private institutions have, on average, the highest instructional expenditures per student. Conversely, two-year publics and lower-priced private institutions generally spend the least per student. Among private institutions, per-student instructional expenditures increase as tuition levels rise. On the public side, these expenditures increase with institutional prestige and selectivity.

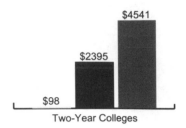

Two-Year Colleges

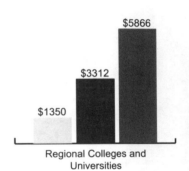

Regional Colleges and Universities

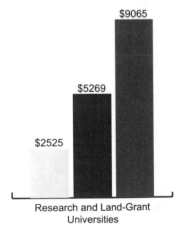

Research and Land-Grant Universities

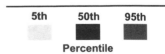

5th   50th   95th

Percentile

PRIVATE

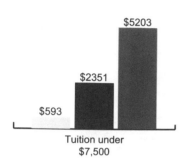

$5203
$2351
$593

Tuition under
$7,500

QUESTIONS

1. What are our instructional expenditures per student?
2. How does this compare with our peer institutions?
3. Is this amount increasing or decreasing over time? What is the reason for any change?
4. How is the amount we spend on instruction determined? Is this amount adequate?
5. What other amounts are included in instructional expenditures?

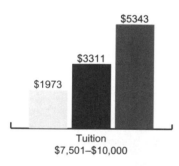

$5343
$3311
$1973

Tuition
$7,501–$10,000

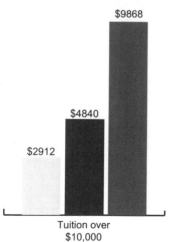

$9868
$4840
$2912

Tuition over
$10,000

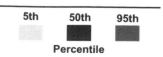

5th	50th	95th

Percentile

Academic Support Expenditures as a Percent of Total Current Fund Expenditures

SIGNIFICANCE

Instruction and other academic pursuits are supported by a host of other activities and resources, such as academic administration, educational media, libraries, and computing. An institution's funding of academic support activities is one reflection of academic quality and represents commitment to current and future achievement.

INTERPRETATION

Private institutions generally spend around 5 percent on academic support activities, and public institutions generally spend between 5 and 8 percent. Public regional colleges and universities and Land-Grant institutions spend, on average, a higher percent than two-year colleges.

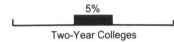

Two-Year Colleges

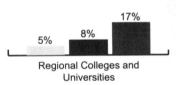

Regional Colleges and Universities

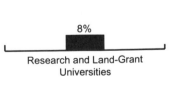

Research and Land-Grant Universities

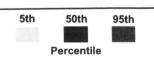

Percentile

PRIVATE

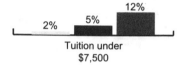

Tuition under
$7,500

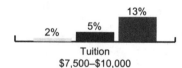

Tuition
$7,500–$10,000

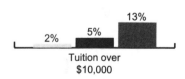

Tuition over
$10,000

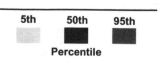

QUESTIONS

1. What percent of current expenditures is devoted to academic support?
2. How does this compare with our peer institutions?
3. Is this amount increasing or decreasing over time?
4. What activities are included in academic support? Are students and faculty satisfied with the quality of these activities?
5. Are academic support activities achieving their goals? Should new activities be added or existing activities be deleted? Should the funding mix change?

Excess (Deficit) of Current Fund Revenues over Current Fund Expenditures

SIGNIFICANCE

An operating excess generally indicates that an institution is meeting its budgetary goals and living within its means. An excess also may reflect an institution's decision to retain a portion of operating revenue for use in future years or to convert a portion of operating revenue to capital. An operating deficit may indicate that an institution is unable to achieve its budgetary objectives. This may be attributable to an unexpected shortfall in revenue, an unexpected increase in costs, or an ineffective budgetary process, notably poor controls and budget monitoring. An operating deficit may also be planned to allow "investments" to improve the quality of present programs or to start new programs.

INTERPRETATION

Survey results indicate that the average institution, whether public or private, balanced its operating budget and ran a slight to substantial surplus in the period studied. On the public side, regional colleges and universities averaged a 6 percent surplus, twice that of the research and Land-Grant universities. Public two-year colleges carried the smallest operating excess, averaging just 1 percent. Among private institutions, the middle-tuition group showed the highest operating surplus, at 7 percent. The low and high tuition groups had surpluses of approximately half that magnitude.

1%

Two-Year Colleges

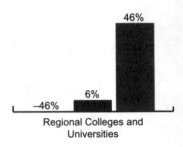

46%

6%

−46%

Regional Colleges and Universities

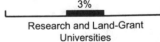

3%

Research and Land-Grant Universities

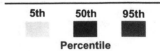

5th	50th	95th

Percentile

PRIVATE

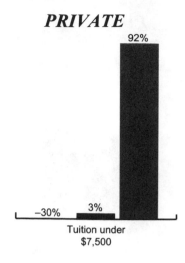

92%

−30%   3%

Tuition under
$7,500

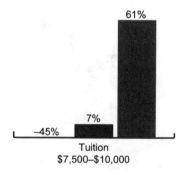

61%

−45%   7%

Tuition
$7,500–$10,000

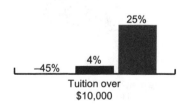

25%

−45%   4%

Tuition over
$10,000

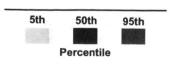

5th   50th   95th

Percentile

<table>
<tr><td></td></tr>
</table>

QUESTIONS

1. What is our operating surplus (deficit)? Was it planned or is it a surprise?
2. How does this compare with our peer institutions?
3. If we are in deficit, what are the causes? What are we doing to ensure that unwanted deficits do not reoccur?
4. If we are in excess, what are we planning to do with the surplus?
5. Do we plan to be in excess or deficit during each of the next five years?

Current Fund Balance This Year as a Percent of Current Fund Balance Last Year

SIGNIFICANCE

Current fund balances represent the operating reserves of an institution. These balances are accumulated over time as the result of excesses in current fund revenues over expenditures. They offer an institution financial flexibility in addressing current needs and unexpected events. Current fund balances as a percent of current fund balances from the prior year measure whether these balances are growing or are being depleted. Some public institutions are not allowed to accumulate fund balances, so this measure will not be meaningful in such cases.

INTERPRETATION

On average, current fund balances increased by about 5 percent from 1990 to 1991, and the amount of increase was relatively similar across institutions. The increase was generally greatest for public institutions, particularly research and Land-Grant universities, where the increase approached 8 percent. These increases suggest that institutions are effectively managing the costs of current operations and preserving operating flexibility.

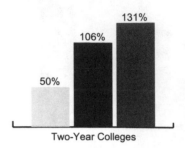

Two-Year Colleges

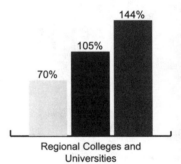

Regional Colleges and Universities

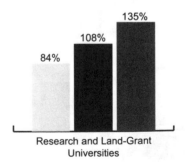

Research and Land-Grant Universities

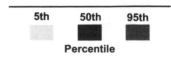

5th	50th	95th

Percentile

PRIVATE

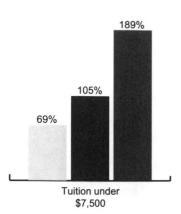

Tuition under
$7,500

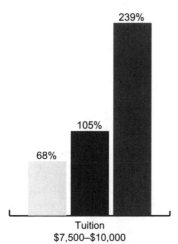

Tuition
$7,500–$10,000

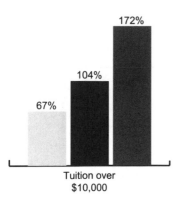

Tuition over
$10,000

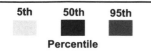

5th   50th   95th

Percentile

QUESTIONS

1. Is our current fund balance increasing or decreasing, and how do we compare to our peer institutions?
2. What are the reasons for changes in our current fund balance? Are these changes planned?
3. Is our current fund balance adequate? What is our policy for setting current fund balances?

Long-Term Debt as a Percent of Total Liabilities

PUBLIC

SIGNIFICANCE

Long-term debt as a percent of total liabilities indicates the importance long-term liabilities assume as a proportion of all liabilities. Generally, long-term debt is incurred for capital projects. Alternatively, short-term debt helps to finance current activities (if debt of any duration is used to fund current operations, this may signal serious problems). Debt is not necessarily "good" or "bad," and it probably should have some place in an institution's capital structure. Too little long-term debt may increase the cost of construction over the long haul. Too much long-term debt may limit an institution's ability to borrow for new programs in the future and may raise the cost of capital for other activities.

INTERPRETATION

About half of all liabilities are long term. The percent of long-term debt is greatest at higher-priced private institutions, where it is nearly two-thirds of all liabilities. This may be due to lesser need for debt to support current activities and greater debt capacity at these institutions. It is lowest at lower-priced private institutions and public institutions, particularly two-year colleges. This may reflect a greater need for funds to finance current activities at these institutions.

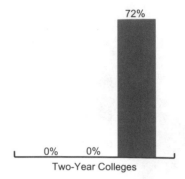

Two-Year Colleges

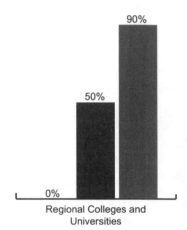

Regional Colleges and Universities

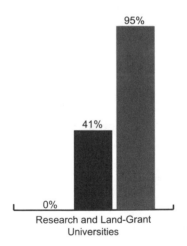

Research and Land-Grant Universities

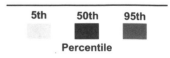

Percentile

28

PRIVATE

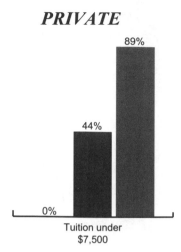

Tuition under
$7,500

QUESTIONS

1. What is our proportion of long-term debt to total liabilities, and how do we compare with our peer institutions?
2. For what purpose have we incurred long-term and short-term debt?
3. What is our debt capacity? Do we have a debt policy?
4. How do we plan to fund capital projects in the future?

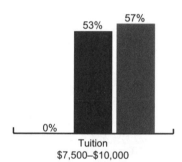

Tuition
$7,500–$10,000

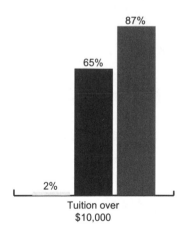

Tuition over
$10,000

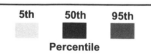

5th   50th   95th

Percentile

Assets as a Percent of Total Liabilities

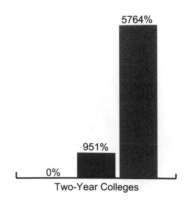

Two-Year Colleges

SIGNIFICANCE

Assets represent the wealth of an institution, and liabilities represent its obligations. The ratio of assets to liabilities is an indication of institutional wealth and the extent to which a school has sufficient assets to cover its liabilities. Generally, the higher the ratio of assets to liabilities, the better off an institution is. This can be deceptive, however, since the greatest slice of assets at most institutions is plant, which in most instances cannot readily be converted to cash. In addition, plant has recurring costs associated with it. Liabilities must eventually be retired, generally from current revenue, gifts, or other revenue in-flows. If these are not adequate, assets must be disposed of to meet debt payments.

INTERPRETATION

On average, assets exceed liabilities by a factor of six to one. This ratio is generally greater for public institutions than private institutions, most likely because public institutions financed some of these capital projects through appropriations and henceforth incurred less debt.

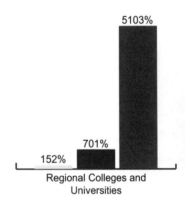

Regional Colleges and Universities

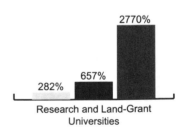

Research and Land-Grant Universities

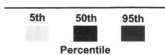

Percentile

PRIVATE

7228%

701%

123%

Tuition under
$7,500

4405%

490%

185%

Tuition
$7,500–$10,000

2296%

432%

185%

Tuition over
$10,000

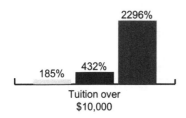

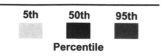

5th	50th	95th

Percentile

QUESTIONS

1. What is our asset-to-liabilities ratio, and how does it compare with our peer institutions?
2. Is the ratio of assets to liabilities increasing over time?
3. What is the composition of our assets and liabilities?
4. Is our level of liabilities appropriate for our level of assets?

Endowment as a Percent of Total Assets

SIGNIFICANCE

Endowment represents institutional wealth and flexibility. Well-endowed institutions have the ability to invest in new programs and to improve the quality of existing offerings. Endowment frees institutions from the constraints of constituents and the vagaries of the marketplace and is a measure of financial strength. Endowment market value as a percent of total assets indicates what proportion of institutional assets is represented by endowment versus plant or other areas.

INTERPRETATION

Endowments represent approximately 20 percent of the wealth of lower- and mid-priced private institutions and 36 percent of the wealth of higher-priced private institutions. More expensive private institutions generally tend to have larger endowments than less expensive institutions. Public institutions often have little or no endowment; however, many public institutions are starting to build endowments, and some have already amassed sizeable endowments.

0%

Two-Year Colleges

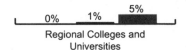

0%   1%   5%

Regional Colleges and
Universities

1%

Research and Land-Grant
Universities

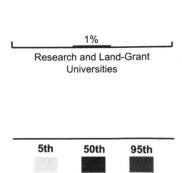

5th   50th   95th

Percentile

PRIVATE

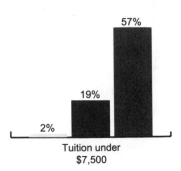

Tuition under
$7,500

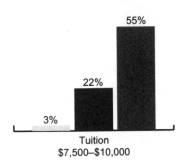

Tuition
$7,500–$10,000

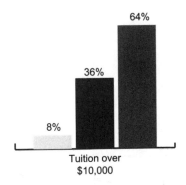

Tuition over
$10,000

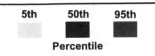

| 5th | 50th | 95th |

Percentile

Endowment per FTE Student

PUBLIC

SIGNIFICANCE

Endowment per FTE student allows apt comparison of the relative wealth and flexibility of institutions. The greater the endowment per student, the more resources are available for investment in instruction, research, and other aspects of learning. Also, institutions with greater endowment per student are less reliant on tuition.

INTERPRETATION

Higher-priced private institutions have the highest endowment per student—nearly $10,000, on average—and more than twice that of mid- and lower-priced private institutions, both of which have, on average, endowments of less than $5,000 per student. Many higher-priced private institutions have endowments per student of between $12,000 and $25,000. Among public institutions a few research and Land-Grant universities have significant per-student endowments. The average two-year public college has no significant endowment.

$0

Two-Year Colleges

$0 $284 $2536

Regional Colleges and
Universities

$0 $1566 $0

Research and Land-Grant
Universities

5th   50th   95th

Percentile

PRIVATE

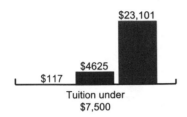

$23,101

$4625

$117

Tuition under
$7,500

QUESTIONS

1. What is our endowment per FTE student, and how does this compare with our peer institutions?
2. Is our endowment per student adequate? Is it increasing or decreasing over time?
3. Do we have a target endowment per FTE student and a specific program for pursuing this goal?

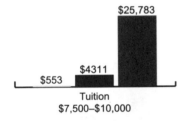

$25,783

$4311

$553

Tuition
$7,500–$10,000

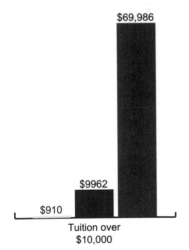

$69,986

$9962

$910

Tuition over
$10,000

| 5th | 50th | 95th |

Percentile

Endowment Yield

SIGNIFICANCE

Endowment yield is the return—the dividends and interest—earned on the endowment during the year and available for expenditure. In part, it is a measure of how well the endowment has been managed. However, yield does not reflect appreciation, and a lower yield may be offset by an increase in appreciation of the endowment during the year (or by prospective gains in the future). Some institutions spend yield and only yield; others use a "payout formula" that permits spending a portion of appreciation when this will not erode the endowment's real value over time.

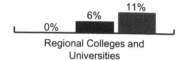

Regional Colleges and
Universities

INTERPRETATION

For the average private institution, endowment yield is generally more than 5 percent and less than 7 percent. Endowment yield for lower-priced private institutions tends to be greater than for higher-priced private institutions. This may be due to lower-priced institutions—which generally have smaller endowments and fewer financial resources overall—adopting possibly riskier investment strategies that yielded higher returns. These institutions might be investing for short-term return rather than long-term growth.

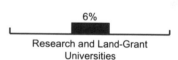

Research and Land-Grant
Universities

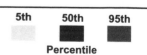

PRIVATE

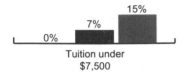

Tuition under
$7,500

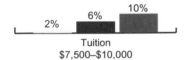

Tuition
$7,500–$10,000

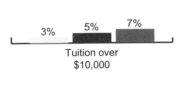

Tuition over
$10,000

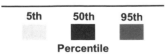

Total Return on Endowment

SIGNIFICANCE

Total return includes interest and dividends earned by the endowment plus appreciation (or depreciation) of endowment assets. Endowments with lower yields often have higher appreciation. Generally, the higher the total return, the better the endowment is performing. However, a lower total return may reflect an investment strategy designed to produce greater future income and appreciation. This strategy also may carry a high risk of capital loss.

INTERPRETATION

Total return for all classes of private institutions is remarkably similar, indicating that endowments of higher-priced private institutions that had lower yields (see Endowment Yield, page 44) largely enjoyed greater appreciation. This also may mean that wealthier institutions with less need for current endowment income were investing for growth—and greater yields in the future. However, one must be cautious when interpreting total return figures for a single year, since returns are known to fluctuate widely over time and across investment strategies.

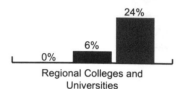

Regional Colleges and Universities

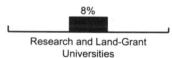

Research and Land-Grant Universities

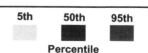

PRIVATE

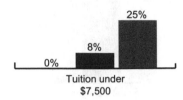

Tuition under
$7,500

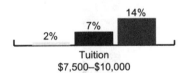

Tuition
$7,500–$10,000

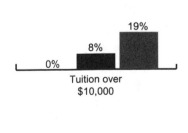

Tuition over
$10,000

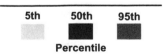

QUESTIONS

1. What is our total return, and how does it compare with our peer institutions?
2. What is our investment strategy? Are we investing more for current yield or appreciation? Are we satisfied with the balance?
3. Should we be plowing some of our yield back into the endowment so as not to erode purchasing power in the future?

End-of-Year Market Value of Endowment as a Percent of Beginning-of-Year Value

SIGNIFICANCE

This indicator measures the annual increase (or decrease) in market value of endowment. In order to preserve the future purchasing power of the endowment so that future generations may also benefit from "perpetual" gifts, endowment market value should increase over time. Market value is increased by reinvesting endowment yield, asset appreciation, and additions to endowment. Endowment market value is determined by institutional spending policy and fund raising as well as investment management and strategy. This indicator measures the annual increase (or decrease) in market value of endowment.

INTERPRETATION

Increases in endowment market value were very consistent among private institutions. Market values increased by about 7 percent on average in the low and mid-tuition groups and slightly less in higher-tuition private institutions. Among public four-year institutions, endowment values increased by an average of 5 percent.

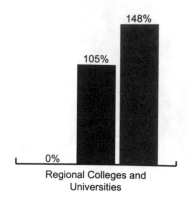

Regional Colleges and Universities

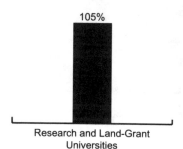

Research and Land-Grant Universities

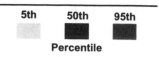

Percentile

PRIVATE

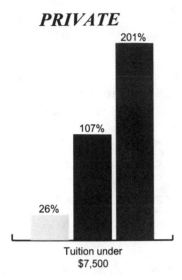

Tuition under
$7,500

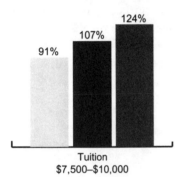

Tuition
$7,500–$10,000

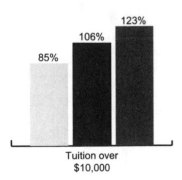

Tuition over
$10,000

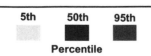

5th	50th	95th

Percentile

QUESTIONS

1. Did the market value of our endowment increase or decrease during the year?
2. Was the change in endowment market value more or less than expected? What accounted for this change?
3. What is our goal for growth of endowment market value? Is this goal realistic? What are our plans to achieve this goal?

Overall Giving

SIGNIFICANCE

The diversity of an institution's charitable giving is a measure of the success of its development activities. A balanced "giving structure" generally reflects a broad range of support for an institution, an integrated development strategy, and the likelihood of stable giving over time. If giving is from relatively few sources, over time it may become a volatile source of revenue. "Unbalanced" giving also may indicate that there are undeveloped opportunities for future giving. A particularly large bequest or capital campaign may disturb the "giving structure" in any particular year. This should, of course, be welcomed, but changes to giving structures that cannot be attributed to identifiable and nonrecurring causes should be examined closely.

INTERPRETATION

Institutions generally have well-diversified development structures. Among public institutions, regional colleges and universities tend to receive a higher proportion of development revenue from annual fund campaigns and other gifts from individuals, and research and Land-Grant universities tend to receive more from corporate gifts and grants. Giving to private institutions is very uniform. Lower-priced institutions tend to receive a slightly smaller percent from annual fund campaigns and slightly more from other gifts from individuals. Higher-priced private institutions tend to receive a greater proportion of support from bequests and foundation awards.

Development Structure

Source	Public Two-year	Public Regional Colleges and Universities AASCU	Public Research and Land-Grant Universities NASULGC	Private Tuition under $7,500	Private Tuition $7,500-$10,000	Private Tuition over $10,000
Annual fund	20%	24%	19%	19%	26%	26%
Other gifts from living individuals	16	22	17	25	21	19
Bequests	6	5	6	9	9	13
Gifts/grants from foundations	8	11	15	16	12	17
Gifts/grants from corporations	24	19	30	11	14	12
Gifts/grants from government	9	8	2	4	9	8
Gifts/grants from foreign government, corporations, foundations	4	--	--	--	--	--
Other gifts/grants	13	10	12	15	8	7

A note about this table. Numbers in this table are numerical averages, or means, in contrast to medians, which are used elsewhere in the book. In a perfectly normal distribution, the median and mean are the same. Where a distribution is highly skewed, the two values may be very different. Hence, the reader will note differences, occasionally extreme, between the values in this table and those found on succeeding pages, where medians of some of the variables that comprise this table are displayed.

QUESTIONS

1. How diversified is our giving, and how does this compare to our peer institutions?
2. Are we too dependent on a relatively few sources of giving?
3. Are gifts from multiple sources increasing or decreasing over time?
4. Are there potentially undeveloped sources of giving that we should be pursuing?

Annual Fund Dollars as a Percent of Total Dollars Raised

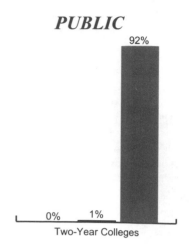

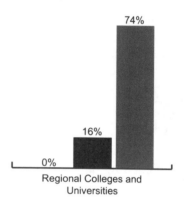

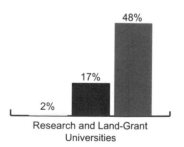

SIGNIFICANCE

Annual contributions support the day-to-day operations of an institution. They are generally unrestricted and often represent one of the largest sources of giving. Annual fund contributions, which indicate the ongoing commitment of alumni and others to an institution, are an increasingly significant part of the revenue structure for many institutions.

INTERPRETATION

Annual fund contributions for mid- and higher-priced private institutions represent, on average, about 20 percent of total dollars raised; for lower-priced private institutions annual fund contributions represent about 11 percent. For public institutions annual fund contributions generally represent around 16 percent of total contributions, except for two-year schools, where they represent barely 1 percent.

PUBLIC

Two-Year Colleges

92%
0% 1%

Regional Colleges and Universities

74%
0% 16%

Research and Land-Grant Universities

48%
2% 17%

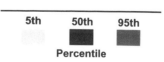

| 5th | 50th | 95th |

Percentile

PRIVATE

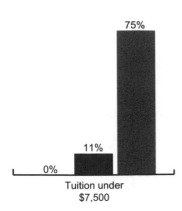

75%

11%

0%

Tuition under
$7,500

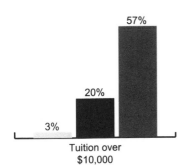

75%

20%

3%

Tuition
$7,500–$10,000

57%

20%

3%

Tuition over
$10,000

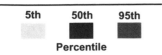

5th 50th 95th

Percentile

QUESTIONS

1. What is our proportion of annual fund giving to total giving, and how does this compare to our peer institutions?
2. Has annual fund giving been increasing or decreasing over time?
3. Is annual fund giving adequate? Are annual fund targets realistic? Should we aim to increase annual giving each year?

Other Gifts from Living Individuals as a Percent of Total Dollars Raised

SIGNIFICANCE

Other gifts usually include contributions to capital campaigns and other special giving programs. These campaigns are an increasingly significant part of over-all financing for many institutions. Targeted giving programs have been successful for many institutions and are gaining in popularity. They may, however, detract from other giving programs, particularly annual giving.

INTERPRETATION

For lower and mid-priced private institutions, other gifts from living individuals generally represent about 20 percent of total gifts; for higher-priced private insti-tutions they represent about 15 percent. For most pub-lic institutions other gifts from living individuals represent about 16 percent of total dollars raised, except for two-year colleges, where they represent about 3 percent.

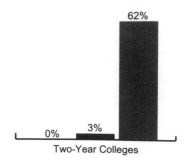

Two-Year Colleges

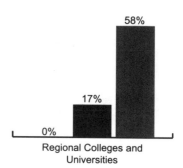

Regional Colleges and
Universities

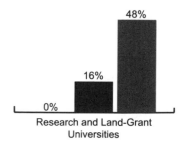

Research and Land-Grant
Universities

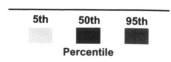

PRIVATE

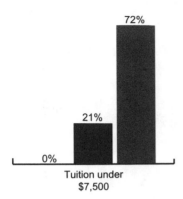

**Tuition under
$7,500**

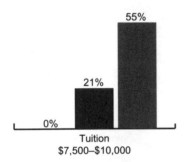

**Tuition
$7,500–$10,000**

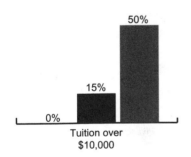

**Tuition over
$10,000**

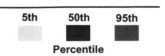

Percentile

QUESTIONS

1. What is our percent of other gifts to total giving, and how does this compare to our peer institutions?
2. What are the components of other giving this year? Why is other giving at this level?
3. How is giving to our capital campaigns and other special giving programs likely to affect overall giving?

Bequests as a Percent of Total Dollars Raised

SIGNIFICANCE

Bequests are a source of significant gifts to many institutions. Often they require considerable research and cultivation by the development staff and substantial investments of time by senior officers and trustees. Receipt of bequests tends to be uneven and unpredictable, so institutions should avoid relying on them to balance the operating budget.

INTERPRETATION

For higher-priced private institutions bequests represent about 7 percent of total contributions; for mid- and lower-priced private institutions they represent, respectively, about 3 percent and 1 percent. For public institutions bequests represent less than 1 percent of total contributions.

PUBLIC

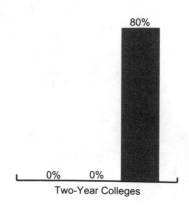

Two-Year Colleges

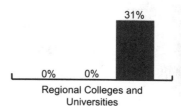

Regional Colleges and Universities

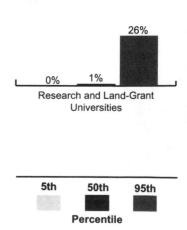

Research and Land-Grant Universities

PRIVATE

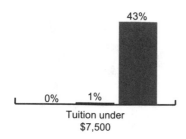

0%   1%

Tuition under
$7,500

QUESTIONS

1. What percent of total gifts are bequests, and how does this compare to our peer institutions?
2. Is our level of bequests increasing or decreasing over time?
3. Do we have a program to identify potential future bequests? Are senior officers and trustees actively involved in pursuing bequests?
4. How do we use money from bequests: for endowment? for facilities? to replenish reserves? or to balance the annual budget?

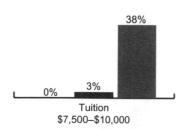

0%   3%

Tuition
$7,500–$10,000

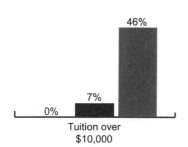

0%   7%

Tuition over
$10,000

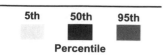

5th   50th   95th

Percentile

Gifts and Grants from Foundations as a Percent of Total Dollars Raised

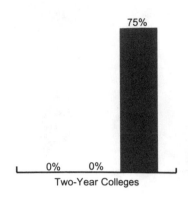

Two-Year Colleges

SIGNIFICANCE

Corporate and private foundations have historically been a major source of university funding. Recently, however, many foundations have turned away from higher education in favor of grants to improve elementary and secondary education and to tackle other social ills. Maintaining foundation funding and improving relationships with foundations is a priority at many institutions. Every effort should be made to channel foundation grants to high-priority institutional programs and to avoid using them to launch new programs that will be burdensome to continue when a grant runs out.

INTERPRETATION

Foundations represent a major source of gifts for research institutions—about 13 percent of total gifts for research and Land-Grant universities and 15 percent for higher-priced private institutions. Foundation support represents about 8 percent of total giving for lower- and mid-priced private institutions and 6 percent for public regional colleges and universities. Two-year schools receive very little foundation support.

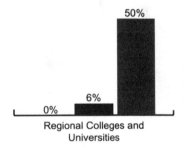

Regional Colleges and Universities

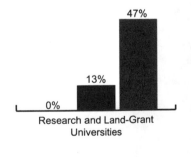

Research and Land-Grant Universities

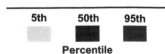

Percentile

PRIVATE

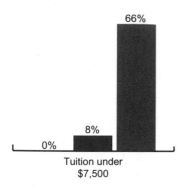

Tuition under
$7,500

QUESTIONS

1. What percent of total gifts are from foundations, and how does this compare to our peer institutions?
2. Is our level of foundation giving increasing or decreasing over time?
3. Are we maintaining our relationships with foundations that have previously supported us? Are we seeking to develop relationships with potential new foundation donors?
4. Are we satisfied with the purposes for which our current foundation grants are used? What can we do to improve the congruence between these grants and our institutional vision?

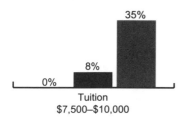

Tuition
$7,500–$10,000

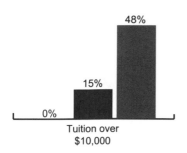

Tuition over
$10,000

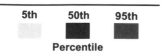

5th   50th   95th

Percentile

Gifts and Grants from Corporations as a Percent of Total Dollars Raised

SIGNIFICANCE

Business, driven by the need for a high-quality work force, is increasingly concerned about education. Corporations tend to give to institutions that offer direct or indirect benefits to them. Frequently, contributions from corporations are taking up the slack from foundations and other traditional donors at many institutions. However, the level of corporate giving is influenced by the state of the economy and tends to diminish during times of recession. Also, competition for corporate donations is intense.

INTERPRETATION

Corporate contributions are a major source of giving to research and Land-Grant universities, where they represent one quarter of all giving. They are also significant for public regional colleges and universities, where they account for over 15 percent of giving. For private institutions corporate giving, on average, is somewhat less prominent, ranging from 6 percent of total giving to lower-priced institutions to 10 or 11 percent at higher-priced institutions.

PUBLIC

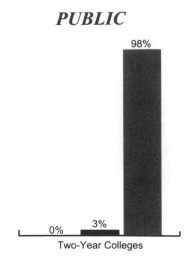

Two-Year Colleges

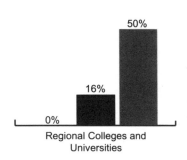

Regional Colleges and Universities

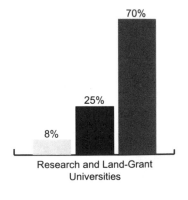

Research and Land-Grant Universities

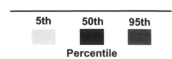

Percentile

PRIVATE

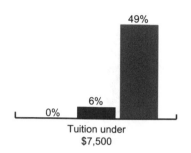

Tuition under
$7,500

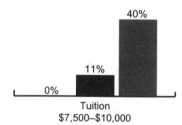

Tuition
$7,500–$10,000

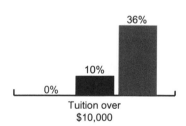

Tuition over
$10,000

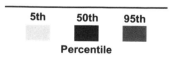

5th 50th 95th
Percentile

Total Restricted Dollars as a Percent of Total Dollars Raised

SIGNIFICANCE

The more unrestricted gifts an institution receives, the greater flexibility it has and, hence, the greater control it can exercise over its destiny. Increasingly, institutions are receiving gifts that are restricted to a specific purpose. Sometimes this is in response to a particular request from an institution, i.e., fund-raising for a new arts center. Often, however, it reflects a donor's desire to designate support for a particular program or activity.

INTERPRETATION

Nearly 70 percent of gifts to institutions are restricted. While this may free current revenue and unrestricted gifts for other uses, it also highlights the limits on the use of resources raised. Money raised by public institutions is far more likely to be restricted—the median is around 90 percent. This may be attributable to highly targeted fund-raising by public institutions and the prospect that unrestricted gifts might revert to the state. Gifts to private institutions are less likely to be restricted than gifts to public institutions. Less than half of the gifts to the median lower-priced private institutions are reported as restricted, rising to more than 70 prcent in high-tuition schools.

PUBLIC

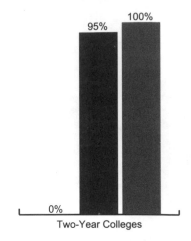

Two-Year Colleges

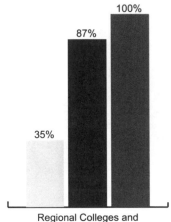

Regional Colleges and Universities

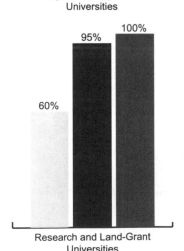

Research and Land-Grant Universities

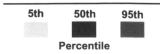

| 5th | 50th | 95th |
Percentile

PRIVATE

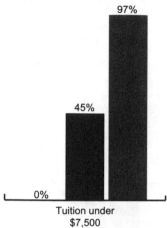

Tuition under
$7,500

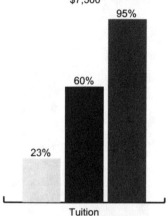

Tuition
$7,500–$10,000

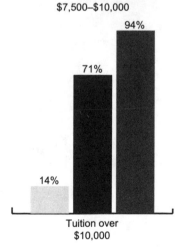

Tuition over
$10,000

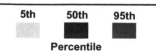

5th	50th	95th

Percentile

Percent of Living Alumni Who Have Given at Any Time During the Past Five Years

SIGNIFICANCE

The higher the percent of alumni who contribute, the greater the participation of graduates in the present and future life of the institution. Alumni are a unique, exclusive, and timeless source of support that must be tended as a valuable resource. Alumni giving is an important proxy for how well an institution is doing—in many cases from those who know it best—and this indicator should be closely monitored.

INTERPRETATION

Overall, about one quarter of alumni contributed to the median institution in our sample. The percentage is highest for private institutions, especially more expensive institutions, where a median of 40 percent of graduates contributed. The median for the research and Land-Grant universities and public regional colleges and universities is roughly one fifth. This is a significant level of giving and represents expanding funding opportunities for public institutions.

Two-Year Colleges

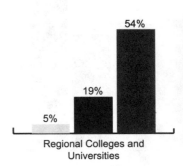

Regional Colleges and
Universities

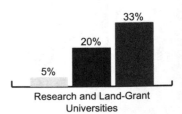

Research and Land-Grant
Universities

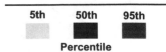

Percentile

PRIVATE

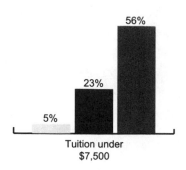

Tuition under $7,500

5% 23% 56%

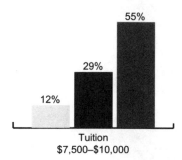

Tuition $7,500–$10,000

12% 29% 55%

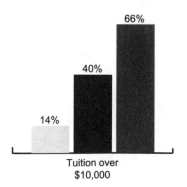

Tuition over $10,000

14% 40% 66%

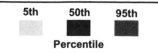

5th — 50th — 95th

Percentile

Physical Capital

Physical capital—buildings, land, and equipment—often receives too much or too little financing, resulting in overbuilding or disrepair. Indicators of operational expenses, new construction and renovations, and deferred maintenance can help institutions monitor trends in physical plant expenditures and better determine when growth or cost containment is necessary.

Plant Operation and Maintenance as a Percent of Current Fund Expenditures

PUBLIC

SIGNIFICANCE

A well-maintained campus helps attract and retain top faculty and students. However, buildings and grounds are expensive to operate and maintain, and there are many competing claims on an institution's budget. It is easy to fall behind on operations and maintenance and create backlogs that will be even more expensive to fund in the future. It also is possible to spend too much in this area and have a plant that, all things considered, is overmaintained. Operations and maintenance expenditures may include amounts for both current and deferred maintenance. Alternatively, operation and maintenance expenditures may be less than needed for current maintenance, increasing the maintenance backlog in the future. Plant operation and maintenance as a percent of current fund expenditures generally shows the level of an institution's commitment to plant.

Two-Year Colleges

INTERPRETATION

On average, institutions spend about 10 percent on operation and maintenance. The exception is research and Land-Grant universities, which spend about one third less. The range is very narrow, with most institutions spending between 9 and 10 percent of current expenditures on operation and maintenance.

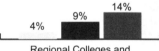

Regional Colleges and Universities

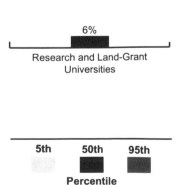

Research and Land-Grant Universities

PRIVATE

QUESTIONS

1. What percent of our current fund expenditures does plant operation and maintenance represent?
2. How does this amount compare with our peer institutions?
3. Is this amount adequate? Is it too much? Is the level of deferred maintenance increasing or decreasing?
4. What are the elements of plant operations and maintenance expenditures?

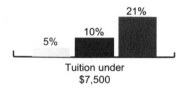

Tuition under
$7,500

Tuition
$7,500–$10,000

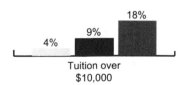

Tuition over
$10,000

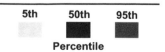

5th   **50th**   **95th**

Percentile

End-of-Year Replacement Value of Plant as a Percent of Beginning-of-Year Value

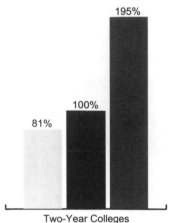

Two-Year Colleges

SIGNIFICANCE

Many institutions continue to construct new buildings despite serious economic problems. At some institutions this is due to the long gestation period between the decision to build and the completion of the building. That is, buildings begun in healthier economic times are only now being completed. Other institutions continue to build due to what is commonly known as the "edifice complex"—the desire to constantly add to plant. Still others build to upgrade technological capabilities, particularly in the sciences. Although new construction generally requires less upkeep than aging plant, new buildings will add to operating and maintenance costs over time. The annual percentage increase in the replacement value of plant (over and above inflation) measures the growth of plant during the year.

INTERPRETATION

Plant expanded, on average, a little over 3 percent. The greatest increase was among the public regional colleges and universities and the mid-priced to more expensive private institutions. The smallest increase was found with less expensive private institutions, public research and Land-Grant universities and two-year colleges. In fact, at two-year colleges the rate of growth was less than one percent, despite rapid enrollment gains.

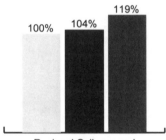

Regional Colleges and Universities

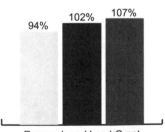

Research and Land-Grant Universities

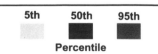

5th   50th   95th

Percentile

PRIVATE

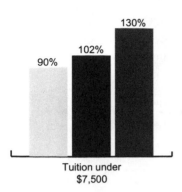

Tuition under
$7,500

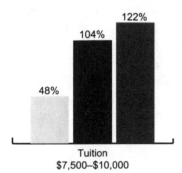

Tuition
$7,500–$10,000

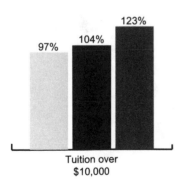

Tuition over
$10,000

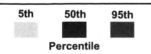

Percentile

QUESTIONS

1. How many new buildings came "on-line" this year? Has replacement cost of buildings increased materially in excess of inflation?
2. Are new building projects currently under consideration? Are these buildings really necessary?
3. What happens to existing buildings that are replaced by new buildings?
4. What is the decision process to construct new buildings or improve existing buildings?

Maintenance Backlog as a Percent of Total Replacement Value of Plant

SIGNIFICANCE

The cost of a building to an institution does not stop once construction has been completed. In fact, during the life of a building, the cost of operations and maintenance often exceeds the cost of construction. During the last two decades many institutions deferred maintenance of their buildings to reduce expenditures and balance their budgets. As a result, many institutions have accumulated significant "deferred" or unmet—and usually unfunded—maintenance. Maintenance backlog as a percent of the total replacement value of plant measures the amount of this deferred cost.

INTERPRETATION

We do not report responses to this question because we believe the data collected were suspect, probably because many institutions have not systematically calculated deferred maintenance at 20 percent or more of total replacement value of plant. Nevertheless, some respondents reported their maintenance backlogs as "zero," a much larger number estimated backlogs of between 2 and 5 percent, and many other institutions did not answer at all. However, some institutions reported quite large values of deferred maintenance, including 20 percent of plant replacement value for the top 5 percent in all institutional categories and more than 50 percent for the top 5 percent of public regional colleges and universities. The "softness" of the responses to this question suggests that many institutions need to give more attention to the accurate estimation of maintenance backlog and, by extension, to plans for financing needed repairs.

QUESTIONS

1. Have we done a systematic study of deferred maintenance, i.e., a comprehensive facilities audit?
2. What is the amount of the maintenance backlog? What is it projected to be next year? In five years?
3. How does the maintenance backlog compare with peer institutions? Is it increasing or decreasing over time?
4. What are the sources of the maintenance backlog?
5. Do we have a plan for reducing the backlog? What is the impact of this plan on other activities?
6. Does funding for plant adequately provide for long-term maintenance, renewal, and replacement?

Information Capital

Institutions must monitor the percent of total expenditures devoted to information capital—libraries and computers—in order to ensure sufficient budget allocations to these fundamentally important, often underfunded learning and research tools. The following indicators offer data on the ratios of books and computers to students, which can help institutions measure the adequacy of their own information resources.

Book and Monograph Volumes per FTE Student

SIGNIFICANCE

Library and other information resources represent an ongoing investment in knowledge. Given the accelerating "knowledge explosion," adequate library resources are essential to learning and research. During hard times some institutions reduce library budgets, and new acquisitions decline. Over time, collections may become dated, and their value to students and faculty diminishes. The number of books and monographs per FTE student provides a relative measure of an institution's investment in library resources. In addition, many institutions are making provisions for acquiring materials through interlibrary loan or "publication on demand" through computer networks in order to better serve students and faculty.

INTERPRETATION

On average, institutions have nearly 80 library volumes per student. Not surprisingly, public research institutions tend to have larger collections and more volumes per student than regional and two-year colleges. In the private sector, collections tend to be largest in high-tuition institutions.

Two-Year Colleges

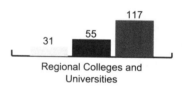

Regional Colleges and
Universities

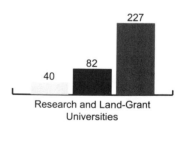

Research and Land-Grant
Universities

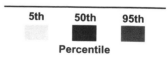

Percentile

PRIVATE

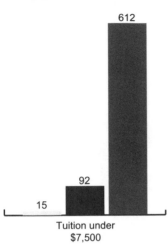

Tuition under
$7,500

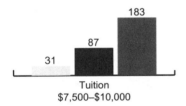

Tuition
$7,500–$10,000

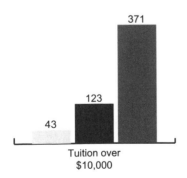

Tuition over
$10,000

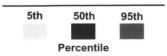

5th	50th	95th

Percentile

QUESTIONS

1. Are the number of book and monograph acquisitions increasing or decreasing annually?
2. How does the library collection compare with the collection of peer institutions?
3. Can we quickly, easily, and inexpensively arrange for the use of materials not in our collection when we need them?
4. Are students and faculty satisfied with the size and quality of library resources?
5. Are library budgets realistic? How are they evaluated? What is the process for increasing or decreasing library budgets?

FTE Students per Microcomputer

SIGNIFICANCE

Technology plays an increasingly powerful role in instruction and research. More and more data are available electronically, and microcomputer skills are critical for data retrieval and analysis. Institutions have made extensive investments in developing and enhancing academic computing capabilities. The number of microcomputers available for students is a measure of an institution's commitment to learning technology. Moreover, forward-looking institutions are amortizing investments in microcomputers over a short enough period to ensure a steady stream of funds for upgrading and replacement.

INTERPRETATION

Institutions generally have one microcomputer for every 22 students. This is remarkably consistent among institution types, ranging from about 14 students per computer at two-year colleges to around 30 students per computer at public regional colleges and universities. Two-year colleges appear to generally have fewer students per computer—this may be attributable to the lack of ownership of microcomputers by two-year college students and the need for institutions to provide them. Among private institutions, those with tuition greater than $10,000 have the smallest number of students per computer.

14

Two-Year Colleges

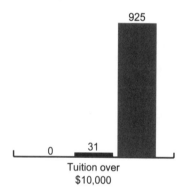

925

0   31

Tuition over
$10,000

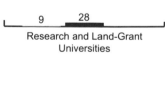

9   28

Research and Land-Grant
Universities

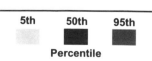

5th	50th	95th

Percentile

PRIVATE

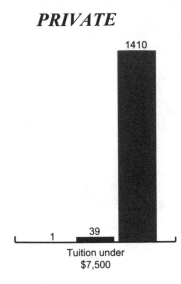

Tuition under
$7,500

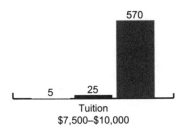

Tuition
$7,500–$10,000

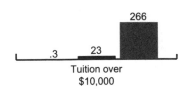

Tuition over
$10,000

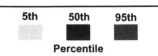

Percentile

71

Human Capital

Students, faculty, and staff are the core of any educational institution. The indicators that follow measure trends in institutional selectivity, ratio of acceptance to matriculation, student-faculty and faculty-staff ratios, faculty tenure, grant aid to students, and other areas related to human resources. Enrollment in particular is central to academic activity and institutional vitality; tracking enrollment indicators can give colleges and universities valuable information on the quality of their own programs and can help them decide whether to undertake improvements or expansions or adjust tuition and financial aid programs to attract and retain more students.

Percent of Total FTE Students Who Are Part Time

SIGNIFICANCE

The population of traditional college-aged students has declined in recent years, and currently the fastest growing segment of the American population is the age 35 and older group. As a result, many colleges and universities have moved aggressively into the market for part-time students, most of whom are working adults. Part-time students affect an institution in a variety of ways. Often they need services tailored to nonresident adults who may have been away from formal education for some time. These students may be more interested in career-oriented programs than their younger, full-time counterparts. And they may alter demand for many of the institution's facilities and services. For example, because it takes several part-time students to equal one full-time student, services such as libraries and student advising facilities may be overtaxed. At the same time, demand for residence halls and traditional student activities may decline as part-time enrollment increases.

INTERPRETATION

Survey data indicate that two-year public colleges enroll far more part-time students than any other institutional segment. This is a predictable finding given the historic mission of community colleges to serve the needs of working adults. Among private colleges, as tuition levels increase, the proportion of students enrolled part time decreases. Because high tuition in the private sector is a proxy for selectivity, these data suggest that pursuit of the part-time student market is a reaction to decreasing demand for full-time enrollment in less selective private colleges.

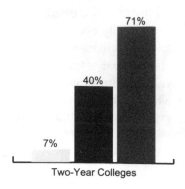

Two-Year Colleges

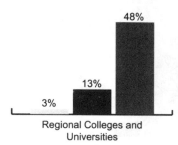

Regional Colleges and Universities

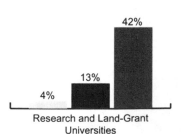

Research and Land-Grant Universities

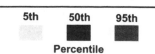

Percentile

PRIVATE

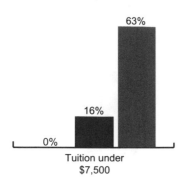

Tuition under
$7,500

QUESTIONS
1. What have been the recent trends in part-time enrollment at our institution?
2. Have changes in part-time enrollment resulted from a conscious institutional strategy?
3. What effects have changes in part-time enrollments had on the use of our facilities and services?
4. Have we altered our program offerings and support services in response to the differing needs and interests of part-time students?

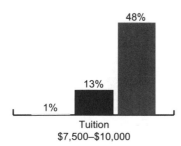

Tuition
$7,500–$10,000

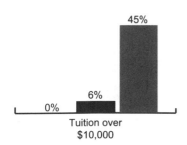

Tuition over
$10,000

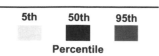

5th	50th	95th

Percentile

Fall 1991 Total FTE Students as a Percent of Fall 1990 Total FTE Students

SIGNIFICANCE

Changes over time in full-time equivalent enrollment can reflect student or institutional choices or a combination of the two. They may signify an increase or decrease in demand by students or potential students caused by factors such as changes in the local population of college-aged students or the success of admissions marketing efforts; inability, especially in the private sector, to meet the financial aid needs of potential students; a conscious effort by the institution to restrict or increase enrollment by altering admission standards; or an alteration in the proportion of full-time to part-time students.

INTERPRETATION

Survey data show slight increases in enrollment in all institutional categories except the high-tuition private groups. Enrollment grew fastest in the two-year public institutions, public regional colleges and universities, and low-tuition private colleges. Overall, these data reflect increasing demand for higher education, despite declines in the population of traditional college-aged students.

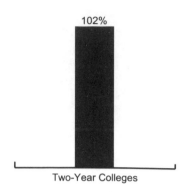

Two-Year Colleges

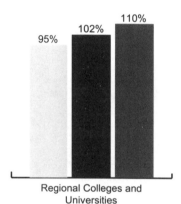

Regional Colleges and Universities

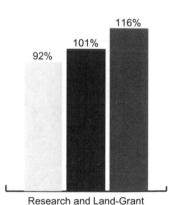

Research and Land-Grant Universities

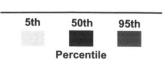

PRIVATE

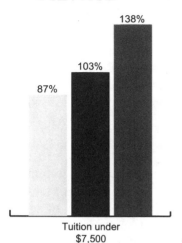

Tuition under
$7,500

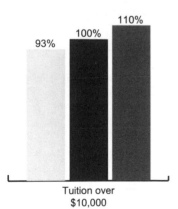

Tuition
$7,500–$10,000

Tuition over
$10,000

5th	50th	95th

Percentile

QUESTIONS

1. What have been the recent trends in enrollment at our institution?
2. What accounts for any changes we have witnessed?
3. How do these changes affect other aspects of our institution, such as the health of our overall budget picture, demand for classes, use of physical plant, and morale of the campus?
4. What steps is our college or university taking to manage the enrollment picture and its effects on the institution?

FTE Enrollment by Racial/Ethnic Status

SIGNIFICANCE

Although colleges and universities are trying to diversify their student bodies, overall minority enrollment still is low relative to the proportion of minorities in the larger population. In general, enrollment by racial/ethnic status may reflect the success of affirmative action programs, the institution's geographical location, the historical and current mission of the institution, and a campus's openness to diversity.

INTERPRETATION

Survey data show that minority students are slightly more likely to be enrolled in public sector institutions. Within the private sector, enrollment of black students drops precipitously as tuition charges rise, but enrollment of Asian-American and Hispanic students tends to increase with rises in tuition charges. Nevertheless, in most institutions, African-American students represent a significantly higher proportion of college and university enrollments than Asian-American, Hispanic, and Native American students combined. Native American students represent under two percent of enrollments in all institutional categories.

QUESTIONS

1. What have been the recent trends in enrollment by racial/ethnic status at our institution?
2. Do these trends reflect conscious institutional efforts, and are we satisfied with these efforts?
3. Do our minority student populations differ systematically from one another and from the majority population in terms of academic preparedness, academic interests, retention, satisfaction with the institution, or other factors?
4. What efforts is the institution making to improve the campus climate for minority students?

PUBLIC

PRIVATE

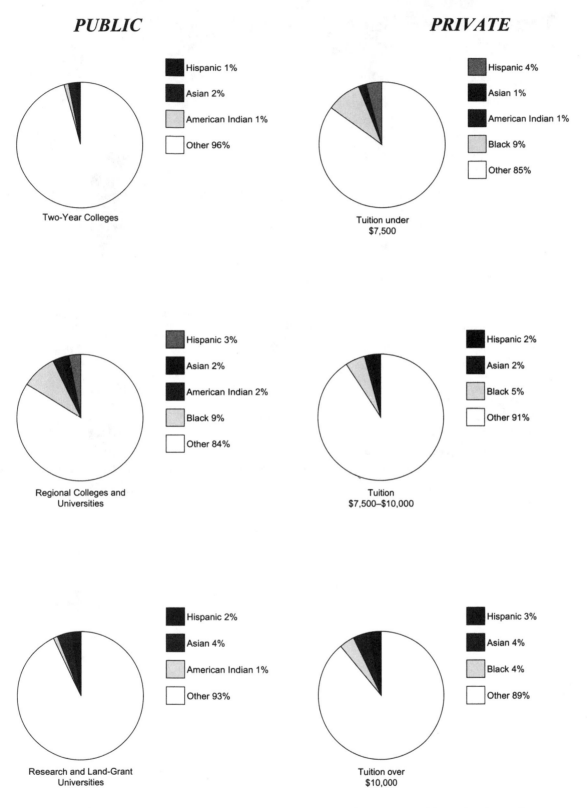

Hispanic 1%
Asian 2%
American Indian 1%
Other 96%

Two-Year Colleges

Hispanic 4%
Asian 1%
American Indian 1%
Black 9%
Other 85%

Tuition under
$7,500

Hispanic 3%
Asian 2%
American Indian 2%
Black 9%
Other 84%

Regional Colleges and
Universities

Hispanic 2%
Asian 2%
Black 5%
Other 91%

Tuition
$7,500–$10,000

Hispanic 2%
Asian 4%
American Indian 1%
Other 93%

Research and Land-Grant
Universities

Hispanic 3%
Asian 4%
Black 4%
Other 89%

Tuition over
$10,000

In some cases the reported figures for African-American students seemed heavily skewed, and therefore they are not reported separately.

Total Female FTEs as Percent of Total FTE Students

SIGNIFICANCE

The number of women in the general population is slightly higher than that of men, a trend that also is evident in the student body of many colleges and universities. Enrollment of women also may be greater because many women are marrying later and entering the work force in larger numbers, making higher education an attractive option. Enrollment by women in higher education has been an important factor in overall enrollment increases for the past several years. Projections by the U.S. Department of Education indicate that enrollment by women in higher education will continue to surpass enrollment by men. However, at some institutions, there may be a conscious effort to manage the ratio of men to women in the student body. Also, a small number of institutions are single-sex, admitting only men or only women.

INTERPRETATION

Survey data indicate that women comprise a majority of total FTE students in all institutional categories, with the highest ratio of women to men found among the two-year public institutions and the lowest-tuition private colleges. In both sectors, as institutional selectivity and costs increase, the percent of women in the student body decreases.

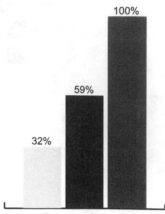

Two-Year Colleges

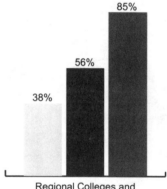

Regional Colleges and Universities

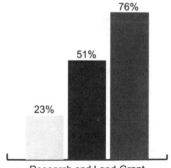

Research and Land-Grant Universities

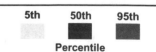

5th   50th   95th

Percentile

PRIVATE

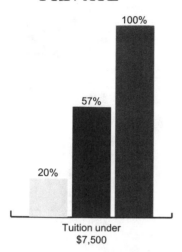

100%

57%

20%

Tuition under
$7,500

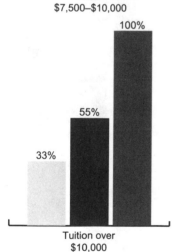

99%

55%

28%

Tuition
$7,500–$10,000

100%

55%

33%

Tuition over
$10,000

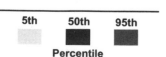

5th	50th	95th

Percentile

QUESTIONS

1. What have been the recent trends in enrollment by women and men at our institution?
2. Do these trends reflect conscious institutional policy or are they coincidental?
3. Do our women students differ systematically from the male student population in terms of academic preparedness, academic interests, retention, satisfaction with the institution, or other factors?
4. Are any changes needed to improve the campus climate (e.g., campus safety) for female or male students?

Percent of Freshman Applicants Accepted

SIGNIFICANCE

The proportion of student applicants accepted by the institution can be affected by a wide range of factors, including admission standards that specify how selective the institution is committed to being; enrollment caps, especially at public institutions whose states and localities are cutting back on financial support; retention rates of upper-class students that affect the number of "slots" available to entering students; availability of nontuition revenues to cushion the effects of enrollment declines; growth or diminution in demand for specific programs the institution offers; availability of financial aid to make enrollment affordable, especially in the private sector; availability of residential and other space on campus to accommodate students interested in enrolling; institutional mission and strategies that define the number and kinds of students who are acceptable; and the level of government financial support provided, especially to public institutions.

An institution may relax its admission standards in order to attract sufficient numbers of students, though in doing so the college may find it must offer more remedial courses, tutoring, and advising, all of which can drive up institutional costs.

INTERPRETATION

Survey data show that public research and Land-Grant universities and public regional colleges and universities are equally selective and that the average two-year college is an open-admissions institution. Within the private sector selectivity increases as tuition rises, reinforcing the conclusion that tuition levels are linked to institutional desirability, status, or real or perceived quality. Except for community colleges, public colleges and universities are more selective than private institutions, perhaps reflecting enrollment caps and inability by many students to afford higher private college tuitions.

PUBLIC

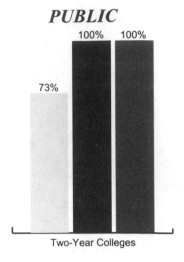

Two-Year Colleges

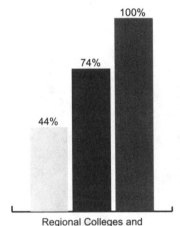

Regional Colleges and Universities

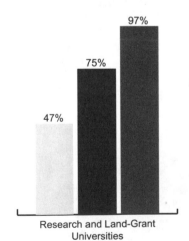

Research and Land-Grant Universities

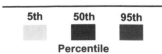

PRIVATE

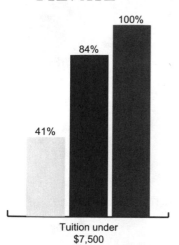

Tuition under
$7,500

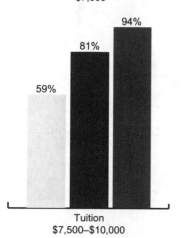

Tuition
$7,500–$10,000

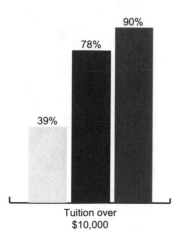

Tuition over
$10,000

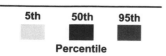

5th	50th	95th

Percentile

Percent of Accepted Freshmen Who Matriculate

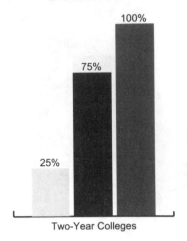

SIGNIFICANCE

The proportion of accepted applicants who actually matriculate is a function of a variety of competitive factors that influence potential students' choices among institutions. These include the relative attractiveness of the institution compared with competitors in terms of program offerings, location, campus facilities, and extracurricular offerings; the number of other institutions to which applicants apply and are accepted; and the total net costs of attending, taking into account the availability of financial aid.

INTERPRETATION

Survey data indicate that accepted freshmen are less likely to matriculate as institutional selectivity rises, whether in the public or private sector. That is, among public institutions matriculation rates are lowest in public research and Land-Grant universities and highest in the community colleges. Within the private sector, matriculation rates decline as tuition/selectivity rises. This finding may suggest that students accepted by selective institutions apply and are accepted by a greater number of schools. It also may suggest in the private sector that as tuition rises, relatively fewer prospective students can afford to enroll.

PUBLIC

Two-Year Colleges

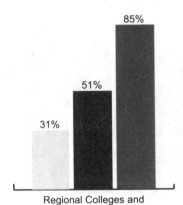

Regional Colleges and Universities

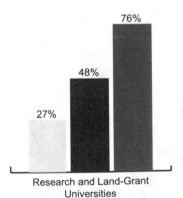

Research and Land-Grant Universities

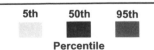

PRIVATE

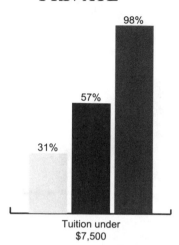

**Tuition under
$7,500**

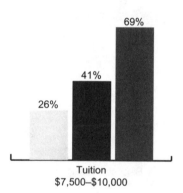

**Tuition
$7,500–$10,000**

**Tuition over
$10,000**

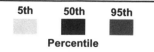

5th	50th	95th

Percentile

QUESTIONS

1. What have been the recent trends in matriculation rates at our institution?
2. What accounts for any changes we have experienced?
3. What would be the long-term consequences of a continuation in our recent matriculation trends?
4. Should we and can we make changes in our policies or institutional practices to increase our matriculation rates?

Percent of Total Students from Outside the U.S. and Canada

PUBLIC

SIGNIFICANCE

American higher education is considered the envy of the world in quality, breadth, and access; and increasingly colleges and universities in this country are attracting students from other nations. Foreign students can shore up enrollments, enhance the diversity of the student body, and preserve institutional financial aid dollars, since these students often pay full tuition. Factors that can influence enrollment by foreign students include the extent to which the institution is known internationally; the institution's aggressiveness in recruiting foreign students; the value of foreign currencies relative to the dollar; the pertinence of the institution's programs to the needs of the home country; the distinctiveness or perceived quality of those programs; and for public institutions, policies that limit enrollment by foreign students or that charge especially high or low tuition and fees to these students.

INTERPRETATION

Survey data indicate that the percent of foreign students tends to increase with institutional selectivity (which also tends to be correlated with institutional visibility and perceived quality). Foreign enrollments are lowest among public two-year colleges, slightly higher among public regional colleges and universities, and higher yet within the public research and Land-Grant universities. Within the private sector, the percent of students from foreign nations is greatest within the middle and high tuition categories.

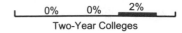

Two-Year Colleges

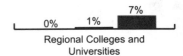

Regional Colleges and Universities

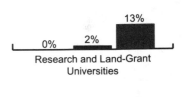

Research and Land-Grant Universities

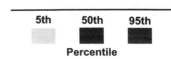

Percentile

PRIVATE

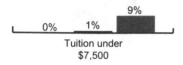

Tuition under
$7,500

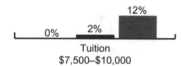

Tuition
$7,500–$10,000

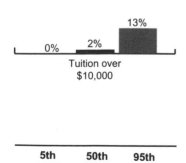

Tuition over
$10,000

Institutional Grant Aid as a Percent of Tuition and Fee Income

PUBLIC

SIGNIFICANCE

Colleges and universities have tended to increase institutional financial aid in order to keep rising tuitions affordable for as many students as possible and to compete with the financial aid packages offered by peer institutions. Institutions that return a high percent of tuition and fees to students in the form of financial aid enhance their ability to attract students and achieve diversity, but often at the cost of diverting funds that otherwise could be available for academic programs. In other words, institutional financial aid reduces tuition revenue (i.e., it discounts tuition).

The policy of tuition discounting may be justified as long as net tuition (gross tuition revenue less institutionally funded financial aid) continues to grow. This indicator should be viewed in conjunction with information about institutional selectivity. Less selective institutions that commit a large fraction of tuition to financial aid may be heading for financial difficulty, since their enrollment is directly dependent on offering tuition subsidies.

INTERPRETATION

Survey data show significant tuition subsidies at both public and private institutions, with subsidies generally higher at less selective institutions. It is important to keep in mind that since public tuitions are generally much lower than those in private institutions, the dollar value of a public-sector subsidy will be much smaller. On a percentage basis, the highest subsidies are found at public community colleges, many of whose students are needy. Subsidies at public research and Land-Grant universities and public regional colleges and universities are somewhat lower. In the private sector the lowest subsidies are found in the middle-tuition group and the highest among the low-tuition institutions. This finding, in combination with the observation that lower-tuition institutions are less selective, suggests that these institutions are using tuition subsidies as a recruitment tool for students they might otherwise not be able to attract. In addition, it

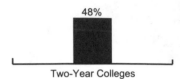
48%

Two-Year Colleges

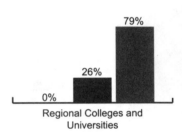
79%

26%

0%

Regional Colleges and Universities

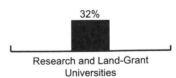
32%

Research and Land-Grant Universities

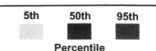
| 5th | 50th | 95th |

Percentile

PRIVATE

probably means that students at lower-tuition institutions are more needy.

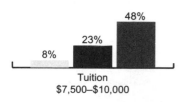

Tuition under
$7,500

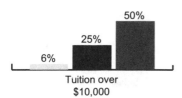

Tuition
$7,500–$10,000

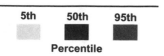

Tuition over
$10,000

QUESTIONS

1. What have been the recent trends in tuition subsidies at our institution? What fraction of the incremental tuition dollar goes to financial aid?

2. What proportion of our tuition discounts come from unrestricted operating funds as opposed to such sources as endowment income or annual giving that are restricted to student aid?

3. What percent of our students are "full pay," and what have been the trends in that figure?

4. What explains our trends in institutional financial aid, and what would be the consequences if they were to continue?

5. Is net tuition revenue growing?

Tuition and Fees per Undergraduate Student (Private) and per In-State Undergraduate Student (Public)

SIGNIFICANCE

Tuition and fee charges are a function of the institution's expenses, its dependence on tuition revenue as opposed to other sources such as private giving or government subsidies, and the target student population's ability to pay. For most colleges and universities tuition is the revenue source most under the institution's direct control, and it tends to be used to fill the gap after other revenue sources have been exhausted. Recently, increases in private-sector tuition have begun to moderate as inflation has decreased and resistance by parents and students to tuition raises has grown. In the public sector tuitions have been rising as a result of cutbacks in state and local support.

INTERPRETATION

Survey data indicate that in the public sector, tuition charges increase with institutional selectivity, with the average charge in research and Land-Grant universities more than twice that of the median community college's tuition. Since data from the private sector are analyzed here according to tuition level, we cannot comment on this indicator for that sector.

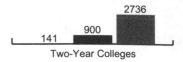

Two-Year Colleges

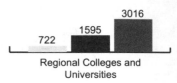

Regional Colleges and Universities

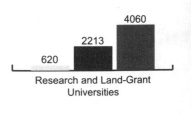

Research and Land-Grant Universities

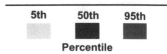

Percentile

PRIVATE

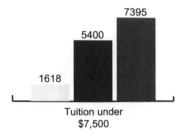

Tuition under
$7,500

1618 5400 7395

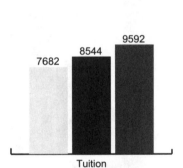

Tuition
$7,500–$10,000

7682 8544 9592

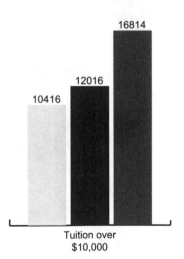

Tuition over
$10,000

10416 12016 16814

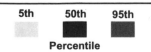

5th 50th 95th

Percentile

Tuition and Fees per Out-of-State Undergraduate Student (Public Institutions Only)

SIGNIFICANCE

Public institutions typically charge higher tuition and fees to out-of-state students in order to compensate for the institution's subsidy by state or local taxpayers. Recent pressure to increase these premiums has grown as state and local economies have faltered and as governments and institutions have increasingly viewed out-of-state students as sources of additional income. However, some selective institutions argue that precipitous increases in out-of-state tuition can lead to a lessening of institutional diversity and overall student quality by discouraging the best out-of-state students from attending the institution. Also, many public institutions located near state borders rely on nearby out-of-state students to keep enrollment levels and overall tuition income high.

INTERPRETATION

Survey data show consistently that premiums more than double the tuition and fees paid by out-of-state students, but that the percent of the increase declines as in-state tuition charges increase. That is, the out-of-state premium is greatest among community colleges and lowest within the public research and Land-Grant universities.

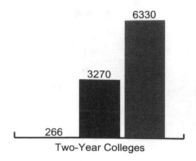

Two-Year Colleges

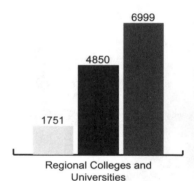

Regional Colleges and Universities

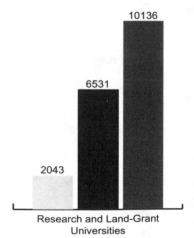

Research and Land-Grant Universities

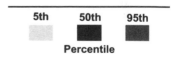

5th   50th   95th

Percentile

QUESTIONS

1. What have been the recent trends in tuition and fees charged to out-of-state students?

2. How dependent is our institution on income from out-of-state students? Is this dependency growing or lessening?

3. Is there a quality differential between our in-state and out-of-state students? In other words, are we dependent on students from other states to shore up the average quality of our student body?

4. What evidence do we have that out-of-state students bring particular forms of diversity to our student body?

5. Is the political climate in our state or locality supportive or hostile to enrollment of out-of-state students?

Percent of Total Students on Institutional Grant Aid

PUBLIC

SIGNIFICANCE

Increasingly, colleges and universities are offering grant aid in order to make tuition affordable to as many students as possible and to compete with the financial aid packages offered by peer institutions. Students who pay full tuition subsidize those who cannot afford the full price. As tuition rises, fewer students are able to pay full tuition and more require subsidies, leading to a spiraling need for institutional financial aid. Institutions that can offer financial aid to a large proportion of their students may be better able to attract and retain those students, but they also may be committing resources to financial aid that could be used for other purposes, such as academic programs, facility improvements, or other needs. Grants that are financed with endowment or other income restricted to financial aid have less impact on the institution's financial position than those paid for with unrestricted current income.

INTERPRETATION

Survey data indicate that in the private sector, the proportion of students with institutional grant aid increases as tuition levels rise. This may suggest that high-tuition institutions have more resources to devote to financial aid, that high tuition makes relatively more students qualified for financial aid, or some combination of the two. In the public sector a much smaller proportion of students receive institutional grant aid, suggesting that more financial aid is received from external sources, that fewer students demonstrate need, or that there is less grant aid available.

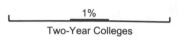

1%

Two-Year Colleges

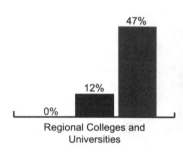

47%

12%

0%

Regional Colleges and Universities

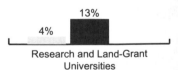

13%

4%

Research and Land-Grant Universities

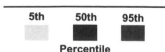

5th	50th	95th

Percentile

PRIVATE

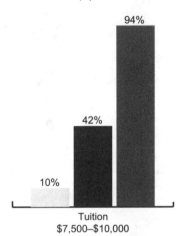

Tuition under
$7,500

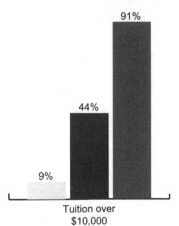

Tuition
$7,500–$10,000

Tuition over
$10,000

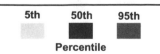

5th	50th	95th

Percentile

QUESTIONS

1. What have been the recent trends in the percent of our students receiving institutional grant aid?
2. What proportion of our grant aid comes from unrestricted operating funds as opposed to such sources as endowment income or annual giving that are restricted to student aid?
3. What explains our trends in institutional grant aid, and what would be the consequences if they were to continue?

Percent of Total Students with Externally Funded Grant Aid

SIGNIFICANCE

Most externally funded grant aid comes from government sources. Such outside aid enables needy students to attend college and prevents the entire financial aid burden from falling on the shoulders of individuals and institutions that could not afford to meet the full financial needs of all students. However, externally funded financial aid is subject to the vicissitudes of the political process, and changes in the availability of aid can significantly affect the ability of colleges and universities to accommodate students interested in attending the school.

INTERPRETATION

Survey data show that on average the percent of students receiving externally funded grant aid is virtually the same in both sectors and all institution types.

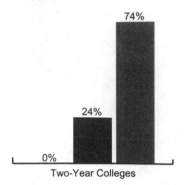

Two-Year Colleges

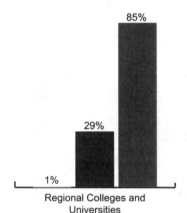

Regional Colleges and
Universities

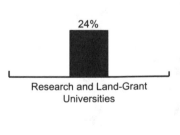

Research and Land-Grant
Universities

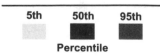

PRIVATE

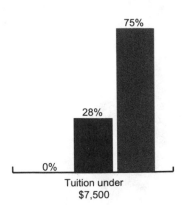

75%

28%

0%

Tuition under
$7,500

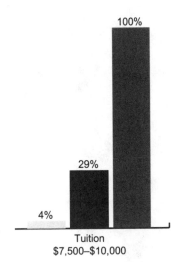

100%

29%

4%

Tuition
$7,500–$10,000

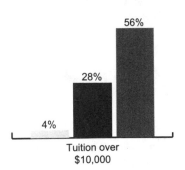

56%

28%

4%

Tuition over
$10,000

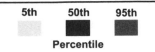

5th	50th	95th

Percentile

QUESTIONS

1. What have been the recent trends in the percent of our students receiving externally funded grant aid?

2. What proportion of external grant aid comes from various sources (e.g., federal government, state government, private sources), and what is our best estimate of future support from each of these sources?

3. What explains our trends in externally funded grant aid, and what would be the consequences if support were to decrease in the future?

Percent of Total Students with Institutional Loans

SIGNIFICANCE

Rather than giving aid outright in the form of grants, some colleges and universities make loans available to students from endowment or operating income. The value of such a program is that needy students receive the funds necessary to attend the institution; but because the funds are paid back, the college can minimize the use of scarce operating funds for grant aid. However, loan programs may put an institution at a competitive disadvantage with other schools that offer grant aid rather than loans to a potential student, and these programs also can be expensive to administer. Moreover, excessive undergraduate loan burdens also may discourage graduates from considering graduate education.

INTERPRETATION

Survey data indicate that very few public or private institutions offer loans to their students, perhaps because in a competitive market for students, grants are far more attractive than loans. Moreover, loans are available from a variety of governmental and private sources, and students who wish to borrow money have options other than the institution.

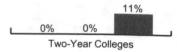

Two-Year Colleges

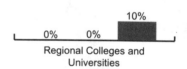

Regional Colleges and Universities

0%

Research and Land-Grant Universities

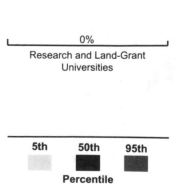

Percentile

PRIVATE

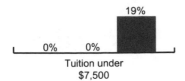

Tuition under
$7,500

QUESTIONS

1. To what extent are institutional loans a factor in the financial aid packages our students receive, and what have been the recent trends?
2. What other sources of loans are available to our students, and what is the extent of the loan burden our students have undertaken?
3. Would an institutionally sponsored loan program be an attractive way for our college or university to decrease our grant burden?
4. Would substituting loans for grants put us at a disadvantage relative to competing institutions?

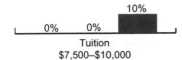

Tuition
$7,500–$10,000

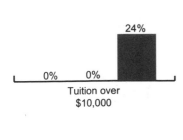

Tuition over
$10,000

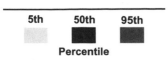

Percentile

Percent of Total Students with Federal College Work-Study Jobs

PUBLIC

SIGNIFICANCE

The percent of students who finance part of tuition and other costs through College Work-Study (CWS) employment is an indicator of the financial need of the student population relative to the costs of attending the institution. The more students who qualify for CWS and hold CWS jobs, the greater the relative need. A higher percent of participation may also reflect the availability of CWS funds, an institution's success in creating positions and integrating students into the work force, and an institution's reliance on student employment to staff needed functions.

INTERPRETATION

Survey data show that within both the public and private sectors, the percent of students with College Work-Study jobs increases as tuition rises. Among private institutions the percent with CWS positions in the highest-tuition category is double that in the lowest-tuition group. Within the public sector the highest percent of students with CWS jobs is found in the public research and Land-Grant universities, which also charge the highest tuition. That CWS employment reflects student need relative to institutional charges is also evident in the fact that the overall percent of CWS-employed students is significantly higher throughout the private sector than in any of the public-sector groups.

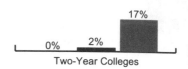

Two-Year Colleges

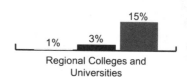

Regional Colleges and Universities

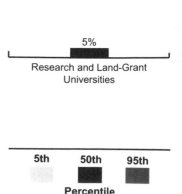

Research and Land-Grant Universities

PRIVATE

Tuition under
$7,500

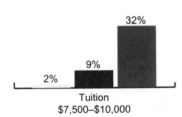

Tuition
$7,500–$10,000

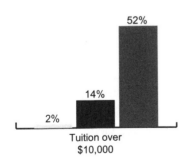

Tuition over
$10,000

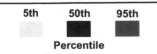

Percentile

QUESTIONS

1. What have been the recent trends in College Work-Study employment at our institution?
2. Are we confident that we have done all we can to maximize the availability of CWS jobs for our students?
3. Have we been successful in parlaying the availability of CWS jobs at our institution into an advantage relative to the institutions with which we compete for students?

Tenure Status of FTE Faculty

SIGNIFICANCE

The percent of faculty who are tenured, nontenured (but tenure-eligible), and nontenure line may reflect the tenure policies and practices of the institution; the presence or absence of tenure quotas; faculty turnover prior to the tenure decision year; the percent of faculty ineligible for tenure (temporary, part-time, and contract faculty, for example); and the retirement and resignation rates of tenured faculty, which at some institutions are being affected by buy-outs and early retirement programs.

As the percent of tenured faculty increases, institutional flexibility, both financial and programmatic, declines. However, tenure quotas can weaken faculty morale by foreclosing opportunities for permanent employment to even the most qualified individuals. Moreover, heavy reliance on temporary and contract faculty may compromise teaching quality and undermine faculty commitment to out-of-class activities such as student advisement and faculty governance.

INTERPRETATION

Survey data indicate that among private institutions, the percent of tenured faculty increases as tuition levels rise. Within the public sector tenure levels are much higher in the public regional colleges and universities and public research and Land-Grant universities than among two-year colleges.

The percent of nontenured (but tenure-eligible) faculty in private institutions decreases as tuition levels rise, suggesting that lower-tuition institutions may be more likely to have younger faculty, tenure quotas, or more turnover among older, tenured faculty. All three public institution groups have approximately the same percent of nontenured faculty.

Within the private sector, the middle- and high-tuition groups are more likely to have nontenure line faculty. Within the public sector, the percent of nontenure line faculty at two-year colleges is nearly twice that of the public regional colleges and universities and also considerably higher than that of research and Land-Grant universities.

QUESTIONS

1. What have been the recent trends in faculty tenure status at our institution?
2. Do we have any explicit or implicit policies or practices that limit the percent of faculty eligible for tenure?
3. Is there any evidence that teaching quality or commitment to advising and other faculty responsibilities varies according to tenure status?
4. If recent tenure and faculty turnover trends were to continue over the next few years, what would be the implications for tenure levels within our faculty? What would be the implications for our budget?
5. What strategies can we adopt to ensure that we maintain necessary financial and programmatic flexibility while maintaining faculty morale and stability?

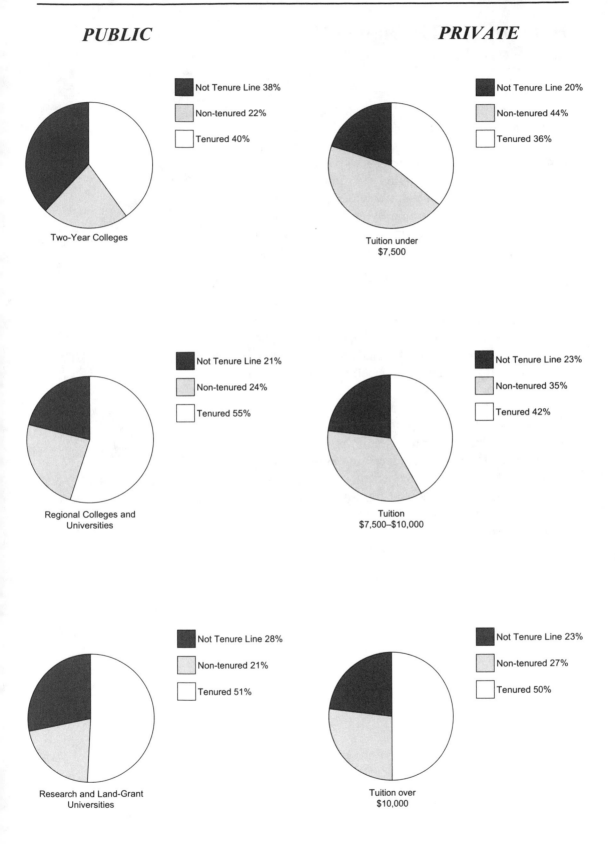

PUBLIC

Not Tenure Line 38%

Non-tenured 22%

Tenured 40%

Two-Year Colleges

Not Tenure Line 21%

Non-tenured 24%

Tenured 55%

Regional Colleges and
Universities

Not Tenure Line 28%

Non-tenured 21%

Tenured 51%

Research and Land-Grant
Universities

PRIVATE

Not Tenure Line 20%

Non-tenured 44%

Tenured 36%

Tuition under
$7,500

Not Tenure Line 23%

Non-tenured 35%

Tenured 42%

Tuition
$7,500–$10,000

Not Tenure Line 23%

Non-tenured 27%

Tenured 50%

Tuition over
$10,000

Percent of FTE Faculty Who Are Part Time

PUBLIC

SIGNIFICANCE

The percent of FTE faculty who are part time may reflect an institutional policy to minimize costs or enhance staffing flexibility by avoiding long-term commitments to faculty; shortages of potential faculty in certain fields; availability of more attractive employment opportunities for potential part-time faculty; a curriculum dominated by technical or professionally oriented programs in which professionals can make important contributions as teachers; and geographic location of the institution insofar as it affects the availability of qualified part-time instructors. Generally, institutions with a higher percent of part-time faculty have lower overall costs for faculty salaries and benefits. At the same time, overreliance on part-time faculty may harm institutional morale, quality of teaching, and accessibility of faculty to students and the institution.

INTERPRETATION

Survey data from the public sector show that dependence on part-time faculty decreases as institutional selectivity rises. That is, the percent of part-time faculty at two-year colleges is nearly three times that of public research and Land-Grant universities. Dependence on part-time faculty within the private sector does not vary a great deal across tuition groupings, though it is lowest in the highest-tuition institutions.

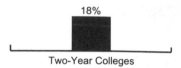

18%

Two-Year Colleges

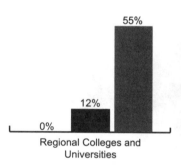

55%

12%

0%

Regional Colleges and Universities

7%

Research and Land-Grant Universities

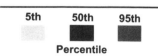

5th	50th	95th

Percentile

PRIVATE

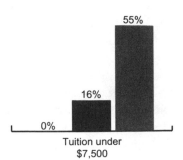

Tuition under
$7,500

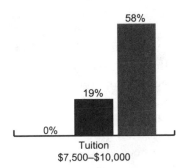

Tuition
$7,500–$10,000

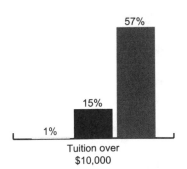

Tuition over
$10,000

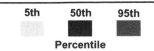

> **QUESTIONS**
>
> 1. What have been the recent trends in employment of part-time faculty by our institution? Do these trends vary by program or department?
> 2. Why do we employ part-time rather than full-time faculty?
> 3. Is there any evidence that teaching quality or commitment to advising and other faculty responsibilities varies by full-time versus part-time status?
> 4. What strategies could we employ to enhance the commitment part-time faculty feel toward our institution and its students?

Ratios of FTE Students to FTE Faculty

SIGNIFICANCE

It is common to describe the productivity of an institution's faculty in terms of the overall ratio of students to faculty. In purely economic terms, a college with a 20:1 ratio is more productive than one whose ratio is 10:1, though it is often argued, accurately or not, that the institution with the lower ratio provides a better education. Institution-wide student-faculty ratios may mask significant variations among programs, departments, or schools within an institution. For example, a university may have an overall ratio of 15:1, but schools within the university may vary between 5:1 and 40:1, depending on student demand for the schools' programs. Ratios can be calculated on the basis of numbers of student majors, as they are here, or according to production of student credit hours. The two measures differ to the extent that faculty in one field provide general education credits or other services to nonmajors.

INTERPRETATION

Among private institutions, survey data indicate that as tuition increases, the average student-faculty ratio declines. Similarly, in the public sector, as institutional selectivity increases, the student-faculty ratio declines. That is, the ratio is highest among two-year institutions and lowest in the research and Land-Grant group. When analyzed by major field, large discrepancies in ratios become evident, though it is important to note again that these data reflect only numbers of majors rather than credit hour production. By far the highest average student-faculty ratios are seen among business programs. Social science ratios are a distant second, followed by science and then humanities.

In general, in the private-sector, ratios are highest in the low-tuition group. Ratios are lowest in the highest-tuition group perhaps because greater resources available to these institutions enable them to hire more faculty. Within the public sector, the two-year college student-faculty ratio for business programs is very high, reflecting the career orientation of many of these institutions. Student-faculty ratios are higher in public regional colleges and universities than in public research and Land-Grant universities, probably reflecting the latter's greater resources and commitment to research.

Ratios of FTE Students to FTE Faculty

Status	Public Two-year	Public Regional Colleges and Universities AASCU	Public Research and Land-Grant Universities NASULGC	Private Tuition under $7,500	Private Tuition $7,500-$10,000	Private Tuition over $10,000
Business	57:1	43:1	32:1	42:1	36:1	34:1
Humanities	22:1	31:1	13:1	12:1	7:1	8:1
Science/Math	23:1	28:1	11:1	12:1	11:1	11:1
Social Science	39:1	45:1	21:1	22:1	19:1	13:1
Overall	59:1	21:1	16:1	19:1	18:1	15:1

QUESTIONS

1. What have been the recent trends in student-faculty ratios at our institution, overall and by program, as well as in terms of majors and credit hour production?
2. Do these trends suggest that we have too many or too few faculty or students in some of our programs? If so, how should we respond?
3. Is there any evidence that particularly high or low student-faculty ratios are having a negative effect on teaching quality, student satisfaction, or faculty morale?

FTE Faculty by Racial/Ethnic Status

SIGNIFICANCE

The diversity of the American population has increased significantly in recent years, and many colleges and universities have been working harder to increase the diversity of their faculty, though numbers of minority faculty on most campuses are still very low. The racial and ethnic makeup of the faculty is a function of the relationship of the institution's program mix to the supply of faculty, the success of affirmative action programs, institutional hiring practices and policies, the institution's geographical location, the historic and current mission of the institution, and the openness of the campus to diversity.

INTERPRETATION

Survey data show that minority faculty, especially African-Americans, are more likely to be found in public-sector institutions. Also within that sector, Asian-American faculty are more prevalent at public regional colleges and universities and research and Land-Grant universities, while Hispanic faculty are more common in two-year colleges. In the private sector, diversity generally decreases as tuition rises, except in the case of Asian-Americans, who are most prevalent in the high-tuition group. Native Americans represent well under one percent of FTE faculty in all institutional categories and thus are not reported here.

QUESTIONS

1. What have been the recent trends in faculty employment by racial/ethnic status at our institution?
2. Do these trends reflect conscious institutional efforts, and are we satisfied with these efforts? If not, what corrective actions can we take?
3. Are the employment experiences of minority faculty at our institution comparable to those of nonminorities? If not, what accounts for these differences?
4. What efforts is the institution making to improve the campus climate for minority faculty?

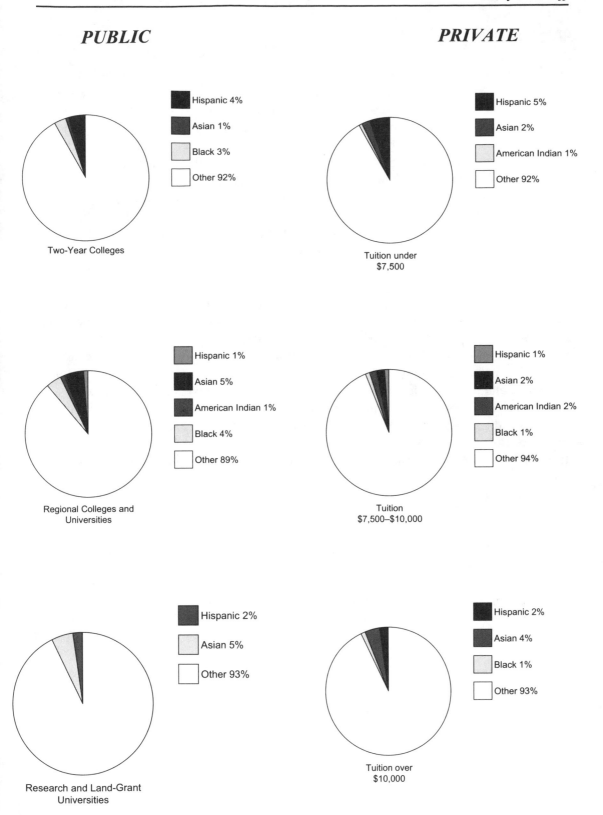

PUBLIC

PRIVATE

Hispanic 4%
Asian 1%
Black 3%
Other 92%

Two-Year Colleges

Hispanic 5%
Asian 2%
American Indian 1%
Other 92%

Tuition under
$7,500

Hispanic 1%
Asian 5%
American Indian 1%
Black 4%
Other 89%

Regional Colleges and
Universities

Hispanic 1%
Asian 2%
American Indian 2%
Black 1%
Other 94%

Tuition
$7,500–$10,000

Hispanic 2%
Asian 5%
Other 93%

Research and Land-Grant
Universities

Hispanic 2%
Asian 4%
Black 1%
Other 93%

Tuition over
$10,000

In some cases the reported figures for African-American students seemed heavily skewed, and therefore they are not reported separately.

Women Faculty

SIGNIFICANCE

The percent of FTE faculty who are women may reflect the hiring policies and practices of the institution, the program mix of the institution in relation to the qualifications of potential women faculty, demand for faculty in fields that historically have attracted larger numbers of women, the success of affirmative action programs, the institution's geographic location, the historic and current mission of the institution, and the openness of the campus to diversity. Once women are hired, their tenure status is a function of the tenure policies and practices of the institution; the presence or absence of tenure quotas; faculty turnover prior to the tenure decision year; the percent of faculty ineligible for tenure (temporary, part-time, contract faculty, and other nontenure line faculty, for example); and the retirement and resignation rates of tenured faculty.

INTERPRETATION

Survey data show that the percent of women faculty has increased substantially in recent years and now averages more than 30 percent across all institution types. The highest concentrations of women faculty are found in public two-year colleges and in the lowest-tuition private colleges. Proportions of women faculty decline as institutional wealth and selectivity increase. Moreover, the percent of women faculty on nontenure lines in both the public and private sectors also increases with institutional wealth and selectivity.

That is, the proportion of women faculty on nontenure lines is highest in the public research and Land-Grant universities and the highest-tuition private institution group. The proportion of non-tenured women faculty in the public sector is highest in regional colleges and universities. Among private institutions, non-tenured women decrease as tuition rises.

QUESTIONS

1. What have been the recent trends in employment and tenure status of women faculty at our institution?
2. Do these trends reflect conscious institutional efforts, and are we satisfied with these efforts? If not, what corrective actions can we take?
3. Are the employment trends and the experiences of women faculty at our institution comparable to those of male faculty? If not, what accounts for these differences?
4. What efforts is the institution making to improve the campus climate for women faculty?

PUBLIC

PRIVATE

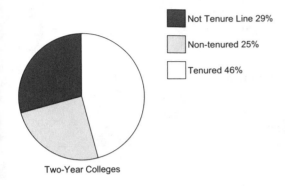

Not Tenure Line 29%

Non-tenured 25%

Tenured 46%

Two-Year Colleges

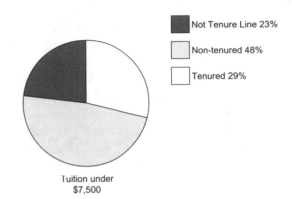

Not Tenure Line 23%

Non-tenured 48%

Tenured 29%

Tuition under
$7,500

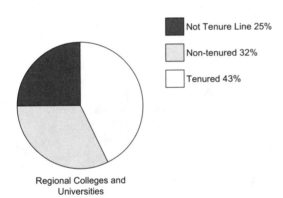

Not Tenure Line 25%

Non-tenured 32%

Tenured 43%

Regional Colleges and
Universities

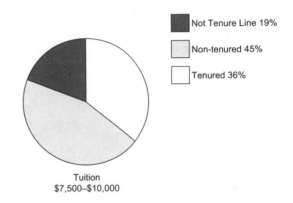

Not Tenure Line 19%

Non-tenured 45%

Tenured 36%

Tuition
$7,500–$10,000

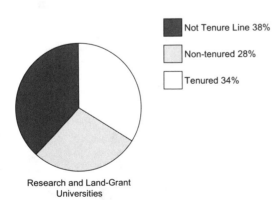

Not Tenure Line 38%

Non-tenured 28%

Tenured 34%

Research and Land-Grant
Universities

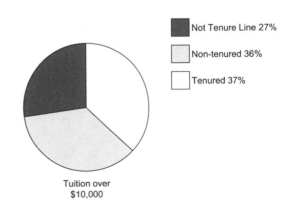

Not Tenure Line 27%

Non-tenured 36%

Tenured 37%

Tuition over
$10,000

Percent of Full-Time Faculty Who Are Older Than 60

SIGNIFICANCE

The percent of an institution's faculty who are older than 60 may reflect institutional retirement policies or government regulations that restrict mandatory retirement; actual retirement patterns; unevenness among age cohorts within the faculty; the presence or absence of retirement incentives and generous pension plans; and an increase or decrease in the hiring of younger faculty. Generally, older faculty earn higher salaries, and so a larger proportion of faculty older than 60 usually means fewer resources will be available for junior faculty.

INTERPRETATION

Survey data indicate that roughly 8 to 11 percent of faculty in all institution groups are older than 60. On average, faculty in the private sector are older than public institution faculty, and two-year public colleges have the fewest number of faculty older than 60.

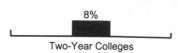

Two-Year Colleges

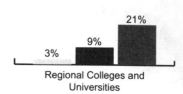

Regional Colleges and Universities

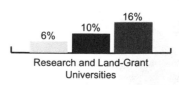

Research and Land-Grant Universities

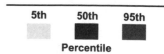

Percentile

PRIVATE

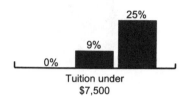

Tuition under
$7,500

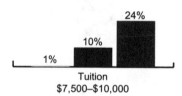

Tuition
$7,500–$10,000

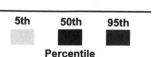

Tuition over
$10,000

<table>
<tr><td>5th</td><td>50th</td><td>95th</td></tr>
</table>

Percentile

QUESTIONS

1. What have been the recent age distributions of faculty at our institution? Do we have more or fewer older faculty than in past years? Are older faculty broadly distributed or concentrated in a few departments?
2. Do we have any explicit or implicit policies or practices that encourage or discourage faculty retirement?
3. Is there any evidence that teaching quality or commitment to research or other faculty responsibilities changes as faculty grow older? If so, how should we respond?
4. If recent faculty age trends were to continue over the next few years, what would be the implications for salary and benefit costs and for employment opportunities for younger faculty?
5. What impact do we expect from changes in federal law governing mandatory retirement?

Total Faculty Head Count at the End of the Year as a Percent of Total Faculty Head Count at the Beginning of the Year

SIGNIFICANCE

Changes in the size of the faculty are a function of hiring practices, the availability of prospective faculty, retirement rates, decisions to grant or deny tenure, and voluntary departures by faculty. In turn, some of these factors are a function of institutional income, changes in overall enrollment levels, student demand for particular programs, and the availability of research dollars to offset some faculty salaries. Because this indicator does not differentiate between full- and part-time faculty, it is possible that numbers of FTE faculty could have changed more than these data suggest.

INTERPRETATION

Survey data show that on average, faculty head count was virtually unchanged during the period studied. Only the public research and Land-Grant universities experienced faculty growth, and that was at modest levels. Because most student enrollments grew slightly during this period, this finding reflects a slight increase in faculty productivity.

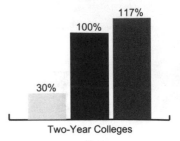

Two-Year Colleges

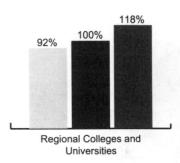

Regional Colleges and Universities

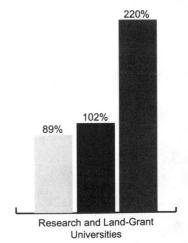

Research and Land-Grant Universities

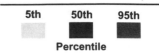

Percentile

PRIVATE

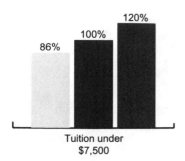

Tuition under
$7,500

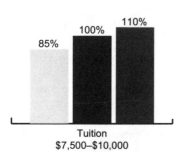

Tuition
$7,500–$10,000

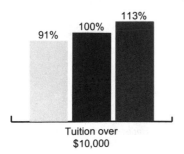

Tuition over
$10,000

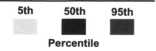

5th   50th   95th
Percentile

QUESTIONS

1. What have been the recent trends in faculty employment at our institution, both in terms of head counts and FTEs?
2. Do these trends reflect conscious institutional policy and practice, or have they occurred more or less by accident?
3. Have changes in faculty employment related in any way to changes in student enrollments? Are there areas where enrollments or other institutional needs suggest we need more or fewer faculty?
4. Have faculty employment trends varied by department, program, or school?

Percent of Total FTE Employees Who Are Faculty

SIGNIFICANCE

The proportion of employees who are faculty reflects the institution's mission and program mix, as well as its choices about the division of labor between faculty and staff. Research-intensive institutions tend to require extra technical and administrative support staff, for example, but other institutions also may choose to leverage faculty time by adding support staff in areas such as student services, admissions, and information technology. Whether such leverage boosts or degrades institutional productivity depends on what faculty do with the time freed up, relative to the school's mission and goals.

INTERPRETATION

Survey data indicate that as institutional wealth and selectivity increase, the proportion of FTE employees who are faculty declines. In the private sector, faculty employment declines as tuition rises. Among public institutions the percent of community college employees who are faculty is more than 50 percent and declines to nearly half that figure in public research and Land-Grant universities, possibly because of their public service and research commitments.

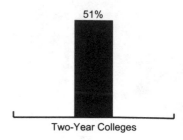

51%

Two-Year Colleges

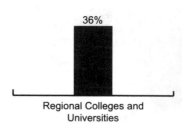

36%

Regional Colleges and
Universities

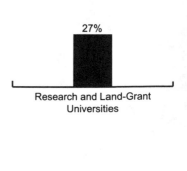

27%

Research and Land-Grant
Universities

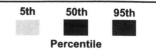

5th	50th	95th

Percentile

PRIVATE

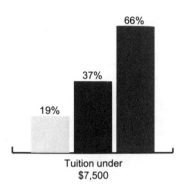

Tuition under
$7,500

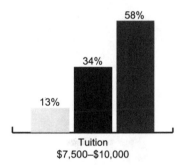

Tuition
$7,500–$10,000

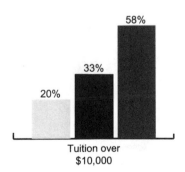

Tuition over
$10,000

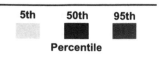

5th 50th 95th
Percentile

QUESTIONS

1. What have been the recent trends in faculty and nonfaculty employment at our institution?
2. In what areas has nonfaculty employment increased or decreased? What explains these changes?
3. If recent employment trends were to continue over the next few years, what would be the implications for our ability to provide instruction, research, and administrative support?
4. Are we satisfied with our faculty-to-staff ratio? How can we begin to make any adjustments that appear to be required?

Academic Unit Staff FTEs as a Percent of Total Staff FTEs

PUBLIC

SIGNIFICANCE

This indicator reflects the extent to which staff (non-faculty) positions are used to directly support academic programs, as opposed to being housed in central organizational units. Differences may be due to policy choices with respect to centralization versus decentralization, but they also can reflect differing priorities for central services (e.g., plant maintenance or student services) or, possibly, staff proliferation.

INTERPRETATION

Survey data show that among private institutions, the smallest portion of staff FTEs assigned to academic units is found in the highest tuition group. Rather than suggesting inattention to the academic function, it is more likely that these institutions have more money to spend on administration, plant operations and maintenance, and other nonacademic functions. In the public sector, public research and Land-Grant universities have twice the proportion of total staff FTEs assigned to academic units that either the two-year or public regional colleges and universitiese.

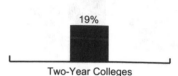

Two-Year Colleges

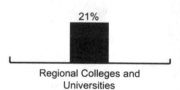

Regional Colleges and Universities

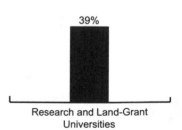

Research and Land-Grant Universities

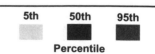

PRIVATE

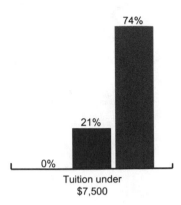

Tuition under
$7,500

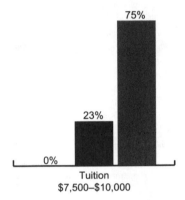

Tuition
$7,500–$10,000

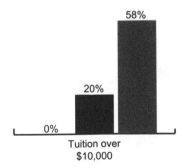

Tuition over
$10,000

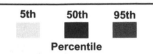

5th	50th	95th

Percentile

QUESTIONS

1. What have been the recent trends in staff employment in academic and nonacademic units of our institution?
2. What explains any changes we have experienced?
3. Are we satisfied that we have deployed staff resources effectively in the pursuit of our mission?
4. If recent staff deployment trends were to continue over the next few years, what would be the implications for our ability to provide appropriate support for academic and nonacademic functions? How can we begin to make any adjustments that appear to be required?

Total Professional and Managerial Staff FTEs as a Percent of Total Staff FTEs

PUBLIC

SIGNIFICANCE

The proportion of staff who are classified as professional or managerial can be a function of the institution's emphasis on administration, oversight, and other professional activities versus functions typically performed by clerical and other nonexempt staff. A high proportion of professional and managerial staff can also indicate that the institution has the relatively greater financial ability required to pay the higher salaries associated with professional and managerial positions or that the complexities of certain institutions require a greater proportion of relatively higher-level staff.

INTERPRETATION

Survey data indicate that as institutional wealth and selectivity increase, the proportion of staff FTEs classified as professional and managerial also increases. In the private sector, professional and administrative staff increase as tuition rises. Among public institutions the percent of community college staff who are professional or managerial is approximately half that found in public research and Land-Grant universities.

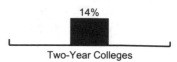

14%

Two-Year Colleges

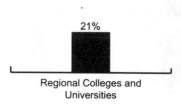

21%

Regional Colleges and Universities

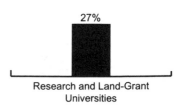

27%

Research and Land-Grant Universities

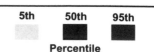

Percentile

PRIVATE

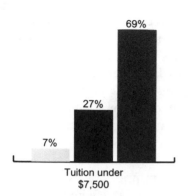

Tuition under
$7,500

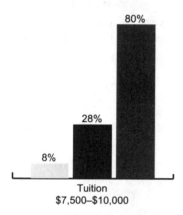

Tuition
$7,500–$10,000

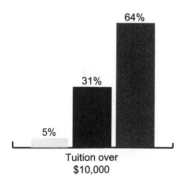

Tuition over
$10,000

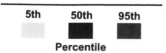

QUESTIONS

1. What have been the recent trends in professional and managerial employment at our institution?
2. In what areas has professional and managerial employment increased or decreased? What explains these changes?
3. If recent employment trends were to continue over the next few years, what would be the implications for our ability to provide appropriate administrative oversight and services? How can we begin to make any adjustments that appear to be required?

Sources of Revenues for Sponsored Research

SIGNIFICANCE

These indicators reflect the extent to which an institution that receives outside research revenues obtains them from the federal government, state and local governments, corporations, and the institution itself. The ability to attract federal funds is a function of the institution's research priorities and capabilities and the extent to which these are consistent with federal needs and programs. Moreover, federal research monies have typically gone to a relatively few large research universities that are especially experienced and adept at competing for funds through federal peer review processes. As a result, some universities have begun to use their political clout to seek earmarked research funding through the legislative appropriations process.

State and local funding typically reflect governmental program priorities as much as institutional initiative and performance. Corporate funding depends on developing close ties with industry. Direct institutional funding usually represents only a small fraction of research support (so-called "departmental research" is included in the instructional expense category). However, the amount of direct institutional support for research may grow as institutions become more accountable for the separate costing of instruction and research.

INTERPRETATION

Survey data show that sponsored research funding is a factor for only a few categories of institutions. In the public sector, more than half of all research dollars received by public research and Land-Grant institutions come from the federal government, nearly 20 percent more than at regional colleges and universities. By contrast, state and local governments are a more significant source of funding for the regional institutions than for the research and Land-Grant universities. For most public institutions, corporations are not a major source of research funding.

In the high-tuition private group, corporations support 14 percent of sponsored research. Moreover, the federal gtovernment and institutions themselves sponsor a significant amount of research in high-cost private colleges and universities. State and local governments are a much less important funding source for these institutions.

QUESTIONS

1. Does our institution receive external support for research? Do we use institutional funds to support research? If so, what have been the recent trends in our receipt and expenditure of these funds?
2. What proportion of our revenues for sponsored research comes from various sources? Have these proportions changed over time?
3. What accounts for any changes we have experienced in recent years in our ability to compete successfully for research dollars?
4. What are our long-term prospects for receiving research funding in the future?

PUBLIC

PRIVATE

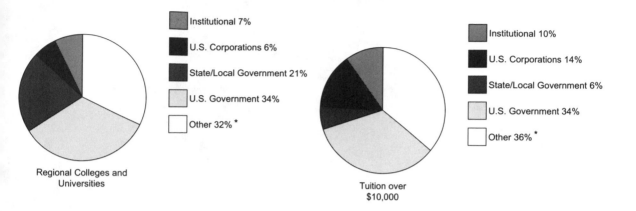

Regional Colleges and
Universities

	Institutional 7%
	U.S. Corporations 6%
	State/Local Government 21%
	U.S. Government 34%
	Other 32% *

Tuition over
$10,000

	Institutional 10%
	U.S. Corporations 14%
	State/Local Government 6%
	U.S. Government 34%
	Other 36% *

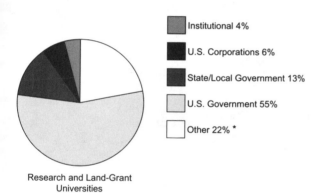

Research and Land-Grant
Universities

	Institutional 4%
	U.S. Corporations 6%
	State/Local Government 13%
	U.S. Government 55%
	Other 22% *

*Includes private foundations, foreign corporations, foreign governments, bequests,
individual gifts, and other sources.

123

Additional Indicators

The following indicators will be of interest to fewer institutions and thus are provided without commentary.

Fall 1991 Total FTE Graduate Students as a Percent of Fall 1990 Total FTE Graduate Students

PRIVATE

PUBLIC

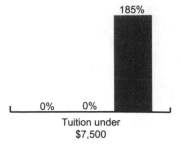

185%

0%   0%

Tuition under
$7,500

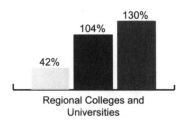

130%

104%

42%

Regional Colleges and
Universities

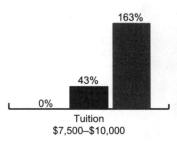

163%

43%

0%

Tuition
$7,500–$10,000

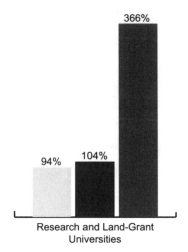

366%

94%   104%

Research and Land-Grant
Universities

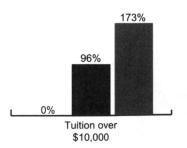

173%

96%

0%

Tuition over
$10,000

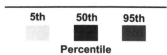

5th   50th   95th

Percentile

FTE Business Major Undergraduates as a Percent of Total FTE Undergraduates

PUBLIC

PRIVATE

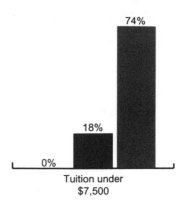

Tuition under
$7,500

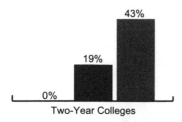

Two-Year Colleges

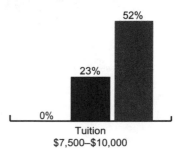

Tuition
$7,500–$10,000

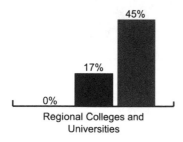

Regional Colleges and
Universities

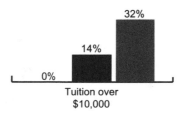

Tuition over
$10,000

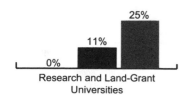

Research and Land-Grant
Universities

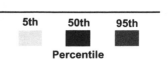

5th   50th   95th

Percentile

FTE Health Profession Major Undergraduates as a Percent of Total FTE Undergraduates

PRIVATE

PUBLIC

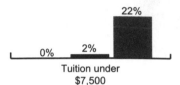

Tuition under
$7,500

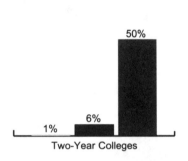

Two-Year Colleges

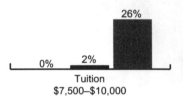

Tuition
$7,500–$10,000

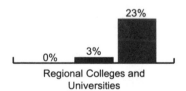

Regional Colleges and
Universities

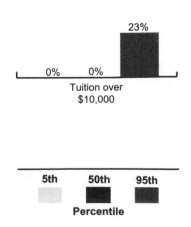

Tuition over
$10,000

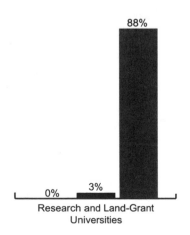

Research and Land-Grant
Universities

5th	50th	95th

Percentile

FTE Humanities Major Undergraduates as a Percent of Total FTE Undergraduates

PRIVATE

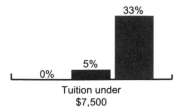

Tuition under
$7,500

PUBLIC

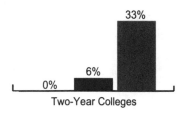

Two-Year Colleges

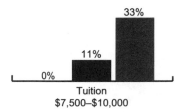

Tuition
$7,500–$10,000

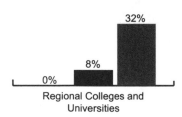

Regional Colleges and
Universities

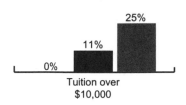

Tuition over
$10,000

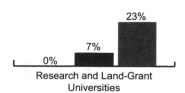

Research and Land-Grant
Universities

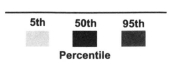

5th   50th   95th
Percentile

FTE Engineering Major Undergraduates as a Percent of Total FTE Undergraduates

PRIVATE

PUBLIC

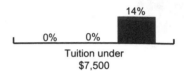

Tuition under
$7,500

0%   0%   14%

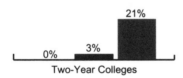

Two-Year Colleges

0%   3%   21%

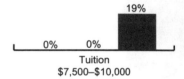

Tuition
$7,500–$10,000

0%   0%   19%

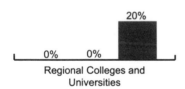

Regional Colleges and
Universities

0%   0%   20%

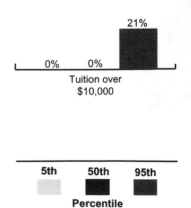

Tuition over
$10,000

0%   0%   21%

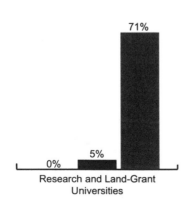

Research and Land-Grant
Universities

0%   5%   71%

5th	50th	95th

Percentile

FTE Science/Math Major Undergraduates as a Percent of Total FTE Undergraduates

PRIVATE

PUBLIC

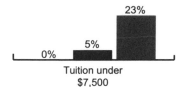

23%

5%

0%

Tuition under
$7,500

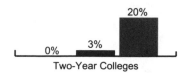

20%

3%

0%

Two-Year Colleges

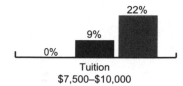

22%

9%

0%

Tuition
$7,500–$10,000

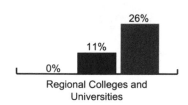

26%

11%

0%

Regional Colleges and
Universities

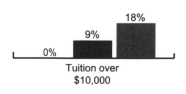

18%

9%

0%

Tuition over
$10,000

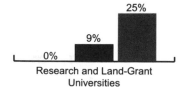

25%

9%

0%

Research and Land-Grant
Universities

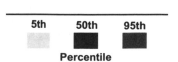

5th   50th   95th

Percentile

FTE Social Science Major Undergraduates as a Percent of Total FTE Undergraduates

PRIVATE

PUBLIC

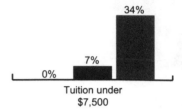

Tuition under $7,500

0% 7% 34%

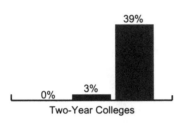

Two-Year Colleges

0% 3% 39%

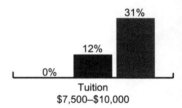

Tuition $7,500–$10,000

0% 12% 31%

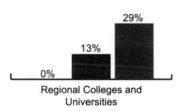

Regional Colleges and Universities

0% 13% 29%

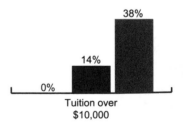

Tuition over $10,000

0% 14% 38%

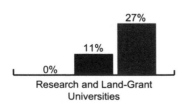

Research and Land-Grant Universities

0% 11% 27%

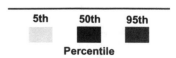

5th   50th   95th
Percentile

Percent of Graduate Applicants Accepted

PRIVATE

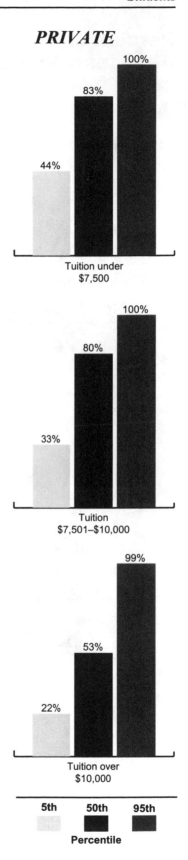

Tuition under $7,500
- 44%
- 83%
- 100%

Tuition $7,501–$10,000
- 33%
- 80%
- 100%

Tuition over $10,000
- 22%
- 53%
- 99%

5th	50th	95th

Percentile

PUBLIC

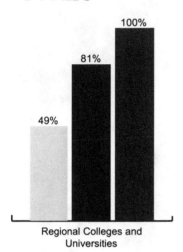

Regional Colleges and Universities
- 49%
- 81%
- 100%

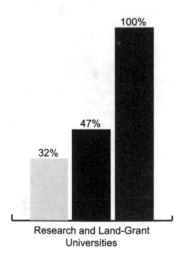

Research and Land-Grant Universities
- 32%
- 47%
- 100%

Percent of Accepted Graduate Applicants Who Matriculate

PRIVATE

PUBLIC

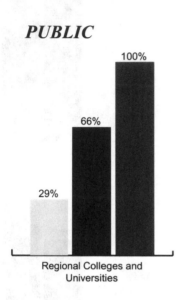

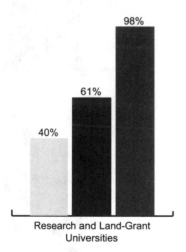

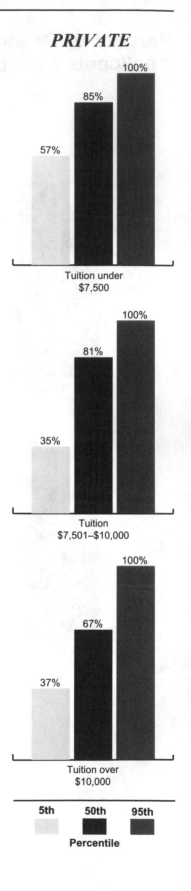

Tuition and Fee Charges per Graduate Student (Private) and per In-State Graduate Student (Public)

PUBLIC

PRIVATE

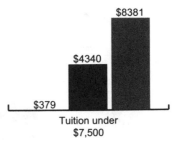

Tuition under
$7,500

$379 · $4340 · $8381

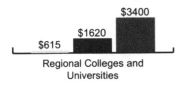

Regional Colleges and
Universities

$615 · $1620 · $3400

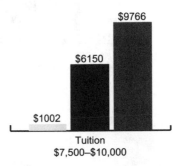

Tuition
$7,500–$10,000

$1002 · $6150 · $9766

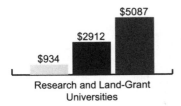

Research and Land-Grant
Universities

$934 · $2912 · $5087

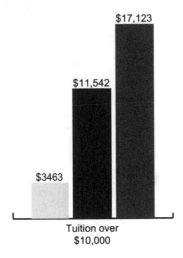

Tuition over
$10,000

$3463 · $11,542 · $17,123

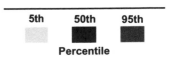

5th	50th	95th

Percentile

135

Tuition and Fee Charges per Out-of-State Graduate Student (Public Only)

PUBLIC

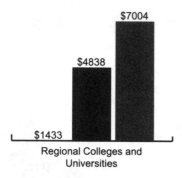

$7004

$4838

$1433

Regional Colleges and
Universities

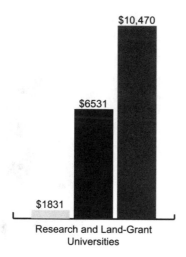

$10,470

$6531

$1831

Research and Land-Grant
Universities

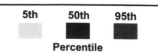

5th	50th	95th

Percentile

Percent of Total Undergraduates on Institutional Grant Aid

PUBLIC

PRIVATE

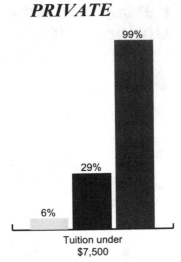

Tuition under
$7,500

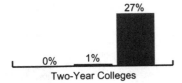

27%

0%   1%

Two-Year Colleges

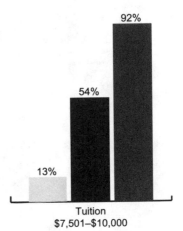

Tuition
$7,501–$10,000

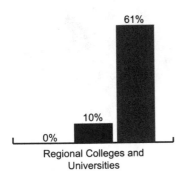

61%

0%   10%

Regional Colleges and
Universities

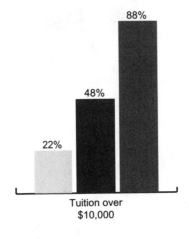

Tuition over
$10,000

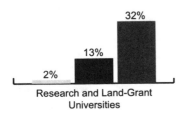

32%

2%   13%

Research and Land-Grant
Universities

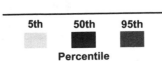

| 5th | 50th | 95th |

Percentile

Percent of Total Undergraduates with Externally Funded Grant Aid

PRIVATE

PUBLIC

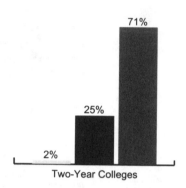

Two-Year Colleges
2% / 25% / 71%

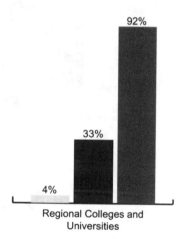

Regional Colleges and Universities
4% / 33% / 92%

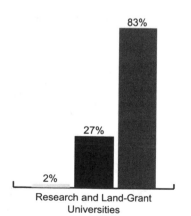

Research and Land-Grant Universities
2% / 27% / 83%

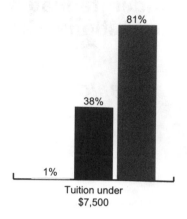

Tuition under $7,500
1% / 38% / 81%

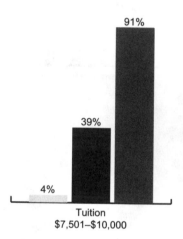

Tuition $7,501–$10,000
4% / 39% / 91%

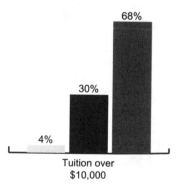

Tuition over $10,000
4% / 30% / 68%

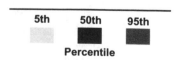

| 5th | 50th | 95th |

Percentile

138

Percent of Total Undergraduates with Institutional Loans

PRIVATE

PUBLIC

Tuition under
$7,500

Two-Year Colleges

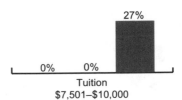

Tuition
$7,501–$10,000

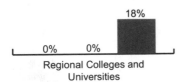

Regional Colleges and
Universities

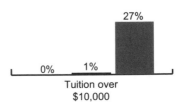

Tuition over
$10,000

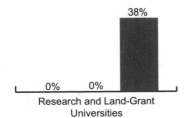

Research and Land-Grant
Universities

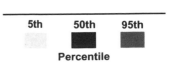

Percent of Total Graduate Students on Institutional Grant Aid

PRIVATE

PUBLIC

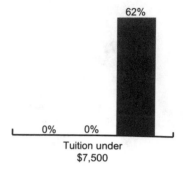

Tuition under $7,500

0% 0% 62%

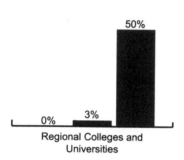

Regional Colleges and Universities

0% 3% 50%

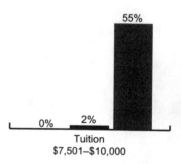

Tuition $7,501–$10,000

0% 2% 55%

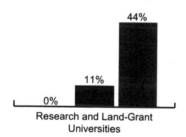

Research and Land-Grant Universities

0% 11% 44%

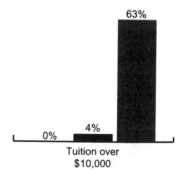

Tuition over $10,000

0% 4% 63%

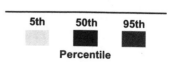

5th   50th   95th

Percentile

Percent of Total Graduate Students with Externally Funded Grant Aid

PRIVATE

PUBLIC

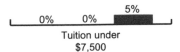

0%   0%   5%

Tuition under
$7,500

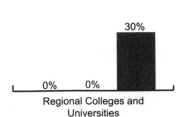

30%

0%   0%

Regional Colleges and
Universities

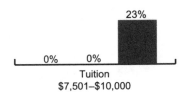

23%

0%   0%

Tuition
$7,501–$10,000

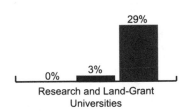

29%

0%   3%

Research and Land-Grant
Universities

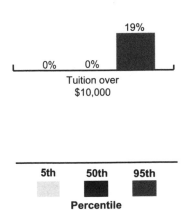

19%

0%   0%

Tuition over
$10,000

5th   50th   95th

Percentile

Percent of Total Graduate Students with Institutional Loans

PRIVATE

PUBLIC

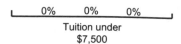

Tuition under
$7,500

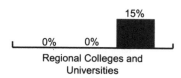

Regional Colleges and
Universities

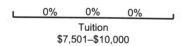

Tuition
$7,501–$10,000

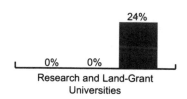

Research and Land-Grant
Universities

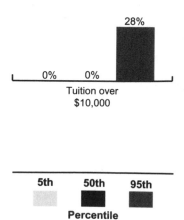

Tuition over
$10,000

142

Percent of Regular Faculty Salaries Offset to Research

PRIVATE

PUBLIC

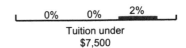

0%   0%   2%

Tuition under
$7,500

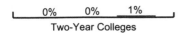

0%   0%   1%

Two-Year Colleges

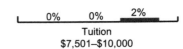

0%   0%   2%

Tuition
$7,501–$10,000

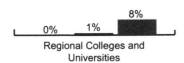

8%

0%   1%

Regional Colleges and
Universities

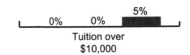

0%   0%   5%

Tuition over
$10,000

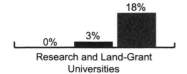

18%

0%   3%

Research and Land-Grant
Universities

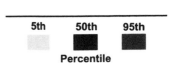

5th   50th   95th

Percentile

NOTES ON THE SURVEY

The indicator values reported in this book are based on the results of a national survey of 1,798 colleges and universities. The survey was mailed in March 1992, followed by a second mailing to nonrespondents in May. The survey was directed to the president's office, with the suggestion that it be completed by the institutional research office or by others with access to the required data.

To help ensure the accuracy of indicator data reported here, we requested raw numbers rather than percentages and calculated the indicators ourselves. The data items included in each indicator and the formula used to calculate it are described in "Calculation of Indicators" beginning on page 147.

Survey response rates, by institution type, were as follows:

Institution Type	Surveys Mailed	Responses Received	Percent Response
Public			
Two-year colleges	292	51	17
Regional colleges and universities[1]	320	121	41
Research and Land-Grant universities[2]	113	46	38
Private			
Tuition under $7,500	429	104	24
Tuition $7,500–10,000	298	130	44
Tuition over $10,000	346	140	40

[1]This category includes colleges and universities eligible for membership in the American Association of State Colleges and Universities.

[2]This category includes universities eligible for membership in the National Association of State Universities and Land-Grant Colleges or the Association of American Universities.

Calculation of Indicators

Indicators and other statistics included in this book were derived or calculated as follows:

Financial Capital

Revenue Structure

Note: Total revenue = tuition and fee income + federal appropriations + state appropriations + local appropriations + federal grants and contracts + state grants and contracts + local grants and contracts + private gifts, grants, and contracts + endowment support for operations + sales and services of educational activities + sales and services of auxiliaries + sales and services of affiliated hospitals + other sources + independent operations

Tuition and Fees as a Percent of Total Revenue: tuition and fee income ÷ total revenue. Page 4

State Appropriations as a Percent of Total Revenue (Public Institutions Only): state appropriations ÷ total revenue. Page 6

Federal Grants and Contracts as a Percent of Total Revenue: federal grants and contracts ÷ total revenue. Page 8

Private Gifts, Grants, and Contracts as a Percent of Total Revenue: private gifts, grants, and contracts ÷ total revenue. Page 10

Endowment Support for Operations as a Percent of Total Revenue: endowment support for operations ÷ total revenue. Page 12

Sales and Services of Auxiliaries as a Percent of Total Revenue: sales and services of auxiliaries ÷ of revenue. Page 14

Expenditure Structure

Note: Total current fund expenditures = expenditures for instruction + sponsored research + public service + academic support + student services + institutional support + plant operations and maintenance + auxiliaries + hospitals + independent operations

Instructional Expenditures as a Percent of Total Current Fund Expenditures: instructional expenditures ÷ total current fund expenditures. Page 18

Instructional Expenditures as a Percent of Total Current Fund Expenditures: instructional expenditures ÷ total FTE students. Page 20

Academic Support Expenditures as a Percent of Total Current Fund Expenditures: academic support expenditures ÷ total current fund expenditures. Page 22

Excess (Deficit) of Current Fund Revenues over Current Fund Expenditures: (total current fund revenues - total current fund expenditures) ÷ total current fund revenues. Page 24

Institutional Grant Aid as a Percent of Tuition and Fee Income: institutional financial aid ÷ total tuition and fee income. Page 88

Resources and Reserves

Note: Total assets = current funds + pure and term endowment book value + quasi-endowment book value + book value of plant + plant funds awaiting investment + equipment book value + designated reserves + other assets

Total liabilities = current liabilities + short-term debt to outside entities + long-term debt to outside entities

Current Fund Balance This Year as a Percent of Current Fund Balance Last Year: current fund balance 1990–91 ÷ current fund balance 1989–90. Page 26

Long-Term Debt as a Percent of Total Liabilities: long-term debt ÷ total liabilities. Page 28

Assets as a Percent of Total Liabilities: total assets ÷ total liabilities. Page 30

Endowment

Endowment as a Percent of Total Assets: total endowment]book value of pure + term + quasi] ÷ total assets. Page 32

Endowment per FTE Student: total endowment ÷ FTE students. Page 34

Endowment Yield: endowment yield ÷ total endowment. Page 36

Total Return on Endowment: total return ÷ total endowment. Page 38

End-of-Year Market Value of Total Endowment as a Percent of Beginning-of-Year Value: end-of-year market value of total endowment ÷ beginning-of-year market value of endowment. Page 40

Development

Annual Fund Dollars as a Percent of Total Dollars Raised: annual fund dollars raised ÷ total dollars raised. Page 44

Other Gifts from Living Individuals as a Percent of Total Dollars Raised: other gifts from living individuals raised ÷ total dollars raised. Page 46

Bequests as a Percent of Total Dollars Raised: bequests ÷ total dollars raised. Page 48

Gifts and Grants from Foundations as a Percent of Total Dollars Raised: gifts and grants from domestic private foundations ÷ total dollars raised. Page 50

Gifts and Grants from Corporations as a Percent of Total Dollars Raised: gifts and grants from domestic corporations and corporate foundations ÷ total dollars raised. Page 52

Total Restricted Dollars as a Percent of Total Dollars Raised: total restricted dollars raised ÷ total dollars raised. Page 54

Percent of Living Alumni Who Have Given at Any Time During the Past Five Years: number of living alumni who have given at any time in past five years ÷ total number of living alumni. Page 56

Physical Capital

Plant Operation and Maintenance as a Percent of Current Fund Expenditures: plant operation and maintenance ÷ total current fund expenditures. Page 60

End-of-Year Replacement Value of Plant as a Percent of Beginning-of-Year Value: end-of-year replacement value of plant ÷ beginning-of-year replacement value of plant . Page 62

Maintenance Backlog as a Percent of Total Replacement Value of Plant: estimated maintenance backlog ÷ total replacement value of plant . Page 64

Information Capital

Books and Monograph Volumes per FTE Student: books and monograph volumes ÷ FTE students. Page 68

FTE Students per Microcomputer: FTE students ÷ number of microcomputers supplied for student use. Page 70

Human Capital

Students

Percent of Total FTE Students Who Are Part Time: total FTE students who are part time ÷ total FTE students. Page 74

Fall 1991 Total FTE Students as a Percent of Fall 1990 Total FTE Students: fall 1991 total FTE students ÷ fall 1990 total FTE students. Page 76

FTE Enrollment by Racial/Ethnic Status:
Black FTE students ÷ total FTE students
American Indian FTE students ÷ total FTE students
Asian FTE students ÷ total FTE students
Hispanic FTE students ÷ total FTE students. Page 78

Total Female FTEs as a Percent of Total FTE Students: total female FTE students ÷ total FTE students. Page 80

Enrollment

Percent of Freshman Applicants Accepted: number of freshman applicants accepted ÷ total number of freshman applicants. Page 82

Percent of Accepted Freshmen Who Matriculate: number of accepted freshmen who matriculate ÷ total number of accepted freshmen. Page 84

Percent of Total Students from Outside the U.S. and Canada: total students from outside the U.S. and Canada ÷ total students. Page 86

Tuition and Financial Aid

Institutional Grant Aid as a Percent of Tuition and Fee Income: total institutional financial aid ÷ total tuition and fee income. Page 88

Tuition and Fees per Undergraduate Student (Private) and per In-State Undergraduate Student (Public): published tuition and fee charges per in-state undergraduate student . Page 90

Tuition and Fees per Out-of-State Undergraduate Student (Public Institutions Only): published tuition and fee charges per out-of-state undergraduate student . Page 92

Percent of Total Students on Institutional Grant Aid: students on institutional grant aid ÷ total students. Page 94

Percent of Total Students with Externally Funded Grant Aid: students with externally funded grant aid ÷ total students. Page 96

Percent of Total Students with Institutional Loans: students with institutional loans ÷ total students. Page 98

Percent of Total Students with Federal College Work-Study Jobs: students with federal work-study jobs ÷ total students. Page 100

Faculty and Staff

Tenure Status of FTE Faculty:
FTE faculty who are tenured ÷ total FTE faculty
FTE faculty who are nontenured ÷ total FTE faculty
FTE faculty who are nontenure line ÷ total FTE faculty. Page 102

Percent of FTE Faculty Who Are Part Time:
FTE faculty who are part time ÷ total FTE faculty. Page 104

Ratio of FTE Students to FTE Faculty:
FTE business students ÷ FTE business faculty
FTE humanities students ÷ FTE humanities faculty
FTE science students ÷ FTE science faculty
FTE social science students ÷ FTE social science faculty
total FTE students ÷ total FTE faculty. Page 106

FTE Faculty by Racial/Ethnic Status:
FTE faculty who are black ÷ total FTE faculty
FTE faculty who are American Indian ÷ total FTE faculty
FTE faculty who are Asian ÷ total FTE faculty
FTE faculty who are Hispanic ÷ total FTE faculty. Page 108

Women Faculty:
FTE faculty who are women ÷ total FTE faculty
female faculty who are tenured ÷ total female faculty
female faculty who are nontenured ÷ total female faculty
female faculty who are nontenure line ÷ total female faculty. Page 110

Percent of Full-Time Faculty Who Are Older than 60: full-time faculty who are over 60 ÷ total full-time faculty. Page 112

Total Faculty Head Count at the End of the Year as a Percent of Total Faculty Head Count at the Beginning of the Year: total faculty head count at end of year ÷ total faculty head count at beginning of year. Page 114

Percent of Total FTE Employees Who Are Faculty: FTE employees who are faculty ÷ total FTE employees. Page 116

Academic Unit Staff FTEs as a Percent of Total Staff FTEs: academic unit staff FTEs ÷ total staff FTEs. Page 118

Total Professional and Managerial Staff FTEs as a Percent of Total Staff FTEs: professional and managerial staff FTEs ÷ total staff FTEs. Page 120

Research

Sources of Revenues for Sponsored Research:
total U.S. government funds ÷ total revenues for sponsored research
state/local government funds ÷ total revenues for sponsored research
domestic corporate funds ÷ total revenues for sponsored research
institutional funds ÷ total revenues for sponsored research. Page 122

Indicators Listed in Back Matter

<u>Students</u>

Fall 1991 Total FTE Graduate Students as a Percent of Fall 1990 Total FTE Graduate Students: total fall 1991 FTE graduate students ÷ total fall 1990 FTE graduate students. Page 126

FTE Business Major Undergraduates as a Percent of Total FTE Undergraduates: FTE business major undergraduates ÷ total FTE undergraduates. Page 127

FTE Health Profession Major Undergraduates as a Percent of Total FTE Undergraduates: FTE health profession major undergraduates ÷ total FTE undergraduates. Page 128

FTE Humanities Major Undergraduates as a Percent of Total FTE Undergraduates: FTE humanities major undergraduates ÷ total FTE undergraduates. Page 129

FTE Engineering Major Undergraduates as a Percent of Total FTE Undergraduates: FTE engineering major undergraduates ÷ total FTE undergraduates. Page 130

FTE Science/Math Major Undergraduates as a Percent of Total FTE Undergraduates: FTE science/math major undergraduates ÷ total FTE undergraduates. Page 131

FTE Social Science Major Undergraduates as a Percent of Total FTE Undergraduates: FTE social science major undergraduates ÷ total FTE undergraduates. Page 132

Enrollment

Percent of Graduate Applicants Accepted: number of graduate applicants accepted ÷ total number of graduate applicants. Page 133

Percent of Accepted Graduate Applicants Who Matriculate: number of accepted graduate applicants who matriculate ÷ total number of accepted graduate applicants. Page 134

Tuition and Financial Aid

Tuition and Fee Charges per Graduate Student (Private) and per In-State Graduate Student (Public): published tuition and fee charges per in-state graduate student. Page 135

Tuition and Fee Charges per Out-of-State Graduate Student (Public Only): published tuition and fee charges per out-of-state graduate student . Page 136

Percent of Total Undergraduates on Institutional Grant Aid: undergraduates on institutional grant aid ÷ total undergraduates. Page 137

Percent of Total Undergraduates with Externally Funded Grant Aid: undergraduates with outside grant aid ÷ total undergraduates. Page 138

Percent of Total Undergraduates with Institutional Loans: undergraduates with institutional loans ÷ total undergraduates. Page 139

Percent of Total Graduate Students on Institutional Grant Aid: graduate students on institutional grant aid ÷ total graduate students. Page 140

Percent of Total Graduate Students with Externally Funded Grant Aid: graduate students with externally funded grant aid ÷ total graduate students. Page 141

Percent of Total Graduate Students with Institutional Loans: graduate students with institutional loans ÷ total graduate students. Page 142

Research

Percent of Regular Faculty Salaries Offset to Research: regular faculty salaries offset to research ÷ total regular faculty salaries. Page 143